EYE-WITNESS

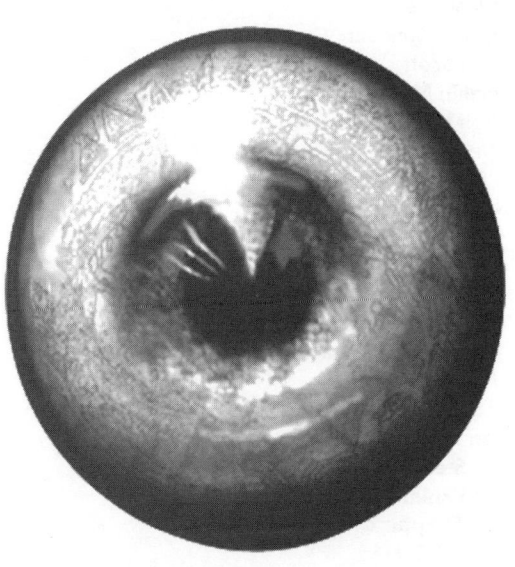

FASA CORPORATION

CONTENTS

WHISTLEBLOWER: A Prologue	4
INTRODUCTION	5
Gamemastering Notes	5
Shadowrun Rules	5
Making Success Tests	6
Success Tables	6
How To Use This Book	6
Preparing the Adventure	6
Plot Synopsis	7
THE ADVENTURE	
A Grave Concern	9
Home Away From Home	13
Vanian's Place	19
Welcome To My Parlor	22
Scene of the Crime	26
Rat's Nest	29
Party Town	32
Black Widow	35
Lion's Den	38
Down In It	44
R.I.P.	48
Early Halloween	53
PICKING UP THE PIECES	59
After the Adventure	59
Karma	59
LEGWORK	60
Electronic Legwork	61
Shadowland	61
People	62
Alpha Blue	62
Clean Steve	62
Dutch Donovan	62
Erin Scott	63
Griffin Moore	63
Iron Legion	63
Neil Scott	64
"Rat" Vanian	64
Places and Events	64
Agrippa and Associates	64
Berkely Management	65
The Cybereye	65
Hammond Necroplex	65
Hammond Massacre	65
Multitech	66
CAST OF SHADOWS	67
Alpha Blue	67
Clean Steve	68
"Rat" Vanian	68
Adam Shepherd	69
PLAYER HANDOUTS	70

EYE WITNESS

Writing
    Mike Nystul

Development
    Tom Dowd

Editorial Staff
    Senior Editor
        Donna Ippolito
    Associate Editor
        Sharon Turner Mulvihill
    Editorial Assistants
        Diane Piron-Gelman
        Rob Cruz

Production Staff
    Art Director
        Jeff Laubenstein
    Project Director
        Joel Biske
    Cover Art
        Rick Berry
    Cover Design
        Joel Biske
    Illustration
        Tom Baxa
        Joel Biske
        Earl Geier
        Darrell Midgetette
    Cartography
        Ernesto Hernandez
        Radley Masinelli
    Layout
        Mark Ernst
    Production Assistant
        Ernesto Hernandez

Published by
FASA Corporation
P.O. Box 6930
Chicago, IL 60680

SHADOWRUN, MATRIX and EYE WITNESS are Trademarks of FASA Corporation. Copyright © 1994 FASA Corporation. All rights reserved. Printed in the United States of America.

Any resemblences in this product between the fictional elements and any real people, corporations, or famous globe-trotting game designers and their work is purely coincidental or satirical in nature (and solely the blame of the author).

EYE WITNESS

EYE WITNESS

WHISTLEBLOWER: A PROLOGUE

Wait for the system to cycle past the hidden camera and then run for the door...

In theory, the break-in should be easy. He'd designed this security system, after all. *Easy in, easy out,* Griffin Moore told himself. *Just follow the plan and stay cool.* Once inside the door and jacked in, his stealth program would do the real work. Griffin suppressed a nervous cough and tried to breathe more slowly. His temples pounded with the agitated rhythm of his heartbeat, and sweat trickled down the sides of his face. Staying cool would be the hard part. Griffin swallowed and forced himself to concentrate on the next step.

Count three and crawl under the invisible IR laser beam without triggering the silent alarm...

Theory was his business. The company employed him as a troubleshooter because he'd written the book on quality control, literally and figuratively. For a brief moment, he wondered what the frag he was doing here. Up until recently he'd been a happy little wageslave, using his talent for computer tech to make a comfortable living. Not exactly ritz, but good enough. And yet here he was ready to chuck it all just because a little something didn't smell quite right. He was a corpboy, born and bred; this shadow drek was out of his field. What kind of fragging hero game did he think he was playing?

Stand perfectly still for thirty seconds, while the program cycles down the motion detector. Keep your hands from shaking, or security will spot you in a heartbeat...

The company valued his work, and paid him well for it. But if the execs had so much respect for his abilities, why had they brushed him off when he told them about the chip? Something felt dangerous-bad, and he had a nasty suspicion what it was.

Wait for the last camera to go dead, then move slowly to the end of the hall...

With a click, the door to R&D swung open, the security system registering the event as an unscheduled maintenance check. Griffin breathed a silent sigh of relief and stepped over the threshold.

He'd only been up to R&D half a dozen times, but he knew the computer system inside and out. It only took him a couple of minutes to find the terminal he needed. Pulling a deck from a nearby work station, he slotted a fistful of custom chips and jacked in.

Sparkling blue and silver, the net stretched out around him in all directions, a spider's web of infinite complexity and unearthly beauty. The cat's cradle of the Multitech system hung in the air before him like a puzzle. If the design team ran their shop by the book, the blueprints Griffin wanted would be archived in a registered datastore; but then again, if everything was frosty, he wouldn't be making this unscheduled visit to the Matrix. Null to registered datastores; he'd have to look elsewhere.

If I were an incriminating file, where would I hide?

Nodes rushed past as Griffin navigated his persona to the datastore that protected the department's secure files. As he approached, a disembodied eye appeared and started scanning for intruders. Griffin spotted it, and with a flick of a mental relay conjured a missile launcher that took out the tracer in a blaze of failing subroutines. A million klicks away, his meat hand wiped a trickle of sweat off of his forehead.

He was in.

In a dark corner of the R&D lab a single screen flickered to life, data flowing in an amber tide across the flatview. Yanking the datajack from his neck, Griffin slid his office chair across the tiled floor, allowing himself a satisfied grin. He'd cross-loaded the file; now he had only to access it to get his answers. Feeling almost carelessly confident at having gotten this far, he triggered an icon, booted the OptiCAD™, and waited as the program interpreted the data he had lifted.

After a few minutes, the OptiCAD™ ceased its low-level grumbling. Griffin stretched in his chair, then leaned forward and began scanning the data. Paging from image to image, he tried to make sense of it with a growing sense of dread. Optical chips were among his specialties, but he had never seen designs like the ones on the flatview. Either some designer had been criminally negligent, or the company was perpetrating a fraud of nightmare proportions.

Griffin swallowed, his mouth suddenly dry. The false confidence of a moment ago drained out of him like air from a popped balloon. If what he was seeing was even half as bad as it looked, he couldn't stop here. He'd have to tell somebody...

His meat body parked in front of a deck across town, a Multitech decker watched Griffin raid the R&D datastore. Whatever was in the restricted file must have meant plenty to the poor slot; the decker wondered if it meant enough to die for. The security code on that particular file called for terminal intervention. He'd jacked in as soon as the flag went up, prepared to burn the poor fragger's brain cells, but the higher-ups had waved him off. He was glad; that meant someone else got to do the wetwork tonight. Handing out terminal brain-fry was the decker's job, but nothing said he had to like it. Shivering, he jacked out and started packing his gear, making a mental note to keep his curiosity to himself.

INTRODUCTION

Eye Witness is a roleplaying adventure set in the world of **Shadowrun**.

The year is 2055. Advances in technology are astonishing, with humans able to blend with computers and travel through that electronic netherworld of data known as the Matrix. Even more astonishing is the return of magic. Elves, dwarfs, dragons, orks, and trolls have reassumed their true forms, while megacorporations (rather than superpowers) rule much of the world. Moving through it all like whispers in the night are the shadowrunners. No one admits their existence, but no one else can do their secret work.

This adventure takes place in the shadows and back alleys of Seattle's urban sprawl. The vast sprawl includes the original city of Seattle and the surrounding sixteen hundred square miles on the eastern shore of Puget Sound. Yet even this vast megaplex is but an enclave set amid even larger states ruled by Native American nations, metahumans, and Awakened beings.

GAMEMASTERING NOTES

Eye Witness nominally takes place in the city of Seattle, but can also take place in any major city the gamemaster chooses. The adventure uses a largely linear story format, with many of its events triggered by actions that the player characters might take in the course of the run. The **Plot Synopsis** in this section summarizes the story background and presents the most probable course of the adventure, though certainly not the only one possible. To run **Eye Witness** the gamemaster needs a thorough familiarity with the contents of this book, and both gamemaster and players should be familiar with the basic **Shadowrun** rules. Except for certain information earmarked as **Player Handouts**, the contents of **Eye Witness** are for the gamemaster's eyes only.

Eye Witness is designed for a team of four to six shadowrunners representing a variety of talent, including at least one mage or shaman and a decker. Players may use any of the character archetypes listed in the **Shadowrun** rules or various supplements, or they may generate their own characters.

SHADOWRUN RULES

Eye Witness uses the **Shadowrun, Second Edition (SRII)** rules. Game information, specifically statistics, appear in the **SRII** format. Gamemasters still using the first-edition **Shadowrun** rules will need to convert the non-player characters (NPCs) presented in this book to their first-edition equivalents. The gamemaster must also adjust weapons for different Damage Codes, watch for differences in some spells, and calculate various Dice Pools for use with the first-edition rules.

INTRODUCTION

MAKING SUCCESS TESTS

During the course of **Eye Witness**, the players will make a number of Success Tests using a skill and a given target number. These tests are indicated by the name of the skill, followed by the appropriate target number in parentheses. For example, a Sorcery (5) Test refers to a Sorcery Success Test against a Target Number of 5.

SUCCESS TABLES

At times, the gamemaster will use success tables to determine how much information the players receive. Each success table lists different information obtained for various numbers of die roll successes. Rolling a higher number of successes always reveals the information listed for lower numbers of successes as well. For example, a character rolling three successes would learn the information for three successes as well as the information for both one and two successes.

HOW TO USE THIS BOOK

Aside from the basic **Shadowrun** rules, this book includes all the information needed to run **Eye Witness**. The gamemaster may also find **The Grimoire, Second Edition** (**Grimoire II**) and **Virtual Realities** (**VR**) useful. Before the start of play, the gamemaster should read through the entire adventure carefully, paying particular attention to the sequence and timing of events. Some important plot developments will not become apparent to the players until well into the adventure, but the gamemaster will have to lay the groundwork for those developments early on. He can best do that by being familiar with the story line. The gamemaster should also carefully examine all maps, plans, diagrams, and player handouts included in this adventure. Where appropriate, the maps are coded with letters that link each area to its description in the text.

Though the written adventure tries to cover all the likely, and even some of the more improbable, events that might occur, it is impossible to foresee every possible action that the players may choose to take. The gamemaster must be prepared to deal with such unexpected actions, and to get the player characters back on track if they stray too far from the beaten path of the adventure.

Eye Witness consists of a number of encounters that describe events the player characters will likely face in the course of this adventure. Most of the encounters contain four sections entitled **Tell It To Them Straight**, **Hooks**, **Behind the Scenes**, and **Debugging**. **Tell It To Them Straight** describes the player characters' location and what is happening to them as though they were actually there. Depending on the actions of the player characters, the gamemaster may occasionally need to adapt the description in **Tell It To Them Straight** to reflect the current situation. Any special instructions to the gamemaster are printed in **boldface** type.

Tell It To Them Straight is followed by a second section, called **Hooks**. This section gives the gamemaster an emotional background to fill out the facts of the encounter, including hints about imagery to use in the scene, emotions to convey, sounds, sensations, textures, and so on. The information provided varies in form and content from scene to scene, ranging from general themes to specific emotions.

Next comes the section entitled **Behind the Scenes**. The real story exists here, and only the gamemaster knows what is really going on at any given moment in the adventure. Straightforward encounters presenting no important plot complications (for example, hiring a vehicle or street samurai and so on) may skip this section. If the players or gamemaster need a map to play an encounter, it appears in this section. Minor non-player character stats needed to roleplay the encounter also appear here, as do suggestions for handling each particular encounter.

Finally, each encounter includes a section entitled **Debugging**. This section suggests ways to get the game back on track if things go too far wrong. For example, the player characters may overlook a vital piece of data, or half the team may meet an untimely death. The suggestions given in this section are just that, however. If he wishes, the gamemaster can ignore these suggestions and let the chips fall where they may.

Several special sections at the end of the book gather together essential information needed throughout the course of the adventure. The **Legwork** section provides information and rumors about various people, places and things that the runners can learn from their contacts or through the public datanets. Statistics for important non-player characters appear in **Cast of Shadows**. Minor non-player character stats appear in the appropriate encounter within the adventure.

Picking Up the Pieces sums up the results of the adventure, depending on the player characters' actions, and provides tips on awarding Karma. **Player Handouts** are documents to be given to the players as their characters find clues and bits of information throughout the adventure.

PREPARING THE ADVENTURE

It is impossible to create a published adventure that provides the appropriate opposition level for every diverse group of player characters. Some groups are inherently more powerful than others.

The gamemaster must adjust the game statistics and capabilities of the opposition to provide an appropriate level of difficulty for his group. If the adventure does not suit the player characters' strengths and weaknesses, the gamemaster may use it as an outline to develop an adventure of his own. Or, if it works well except for a tweak needed here and there, the gamemaster can change any part of the plot and events to make the adventure a better one for his group of players.

This adventure suggests Threat and Professional Ratings for each of the non-player characters. Per the **SRII** rules, use Threat Rating dice in place of Dice Pools for NPCs (p. 187, **SRII**). Gamemasters should adjust the actual Threat Ratings to better reflect the level of opposition presented by the player characters.

Such manipulation will be crucial to running some of the firefights in this adventure at a manageable level. The fights in **Eye Witness** work best choreographed like an action movie. Though lead and magic fly everywhere, only a few of the bad guys actually get a clean shot at the heroes at any one time. That limitation, and the application of the **SRII** Professional Rating rules, should help keep large fights under control.

For gamemasters using the first-edition **Shadowrun** rules, the Professional Rating system works as follows. NPCs with a

INTRODUCTION

Professional Rating of 1 will withdraw from a fight after taking a Light wound. Those rated at 2 will withdraw after taking a Moderate wound, those rated at 3 after a Serious wound, and those rated at 4 will fight until unconscious or dead.

PLOT SYNOPSIS

Though a blessing for some, for many the Awakening proved a living hell. Untiring efforts by metahuman rights groups ameliorated somewhat the plight of disadvantaged minorities such as orks and trolls; though regarded as misfits by much of society, these metatypes escaped the full extent of the metagenic horror experienced by the Sixth World's true outcasts. Of all the Awakened beings, none were more feared or loathed than those humans unfortunate enough to goblinize into ghouls.

Eric Steward is one such unlucky person. Good-looking, intelligent, and born to a life of privilege, Eric had excellent prospects. After graduating from an exclusive prep school, he embarked on a promising career as an investment broker, but lost everything when he goblinized in 2021. The Awakening triggered the time bomb burned into Eric's genetic code; goblinization twisted his body into a wicked parody of its former beauty, making him a ghoul. Once a golden boy with the world at his feet, Eric Steward became a foul, loathsome being that craved human flesh for sustenance and could not bear the sunlight. The shock of the transformation temporarily shattered his mind. For several years, Eric lived in the underworld of the sprawl like an animal; driven by feral bloodlust, he hunted in the shadows and sated his inhuman hunger with human flesh. The little that remained of the man he had been felt horrified by the cannibalism his body now demanded of him, but with each passing year Eric lost a little more of his inward humanity and conscience. In time, he accepted the monster he had become and regained control of both his sanity and his passions. Eventually, Eric disguised his hideous features and left the underworld in search of the justice that the rest of the world had denied his kind. Determined to create a safe haven for his fellow ghouls, Steward turned his formidable intelligence toward finding a way. To finance his crusade, he collected all of the valuables his people had gathered over the years, invested the money, and became a wealthy businessman.

In the early 2050s, the Seattle waste management company **Agrippa and Associates** started showing significant losses. Agrippa held most waste removal contracts for the metroplex of Seattle; in its decline, Eric recognized a golden opportunity. Using the manufactured identity of **Adam Shepherd** and a phony investment group, **Berkely Management**, the ghoul bid for the floundering company, and one way or another made sure that any serious opposition withdrew their offers early.

As Agrippa's new CEO, Shepherd phased out most of the company's human employees, secretly replacing them with ghouls. Because this inhuman workforce received no pay, Agrippa showed impressive growth for the first time in years, reaping Shepherd staggering wealth. Once in a position to look after the needs of his less fortunate brothers, Shepherd established a retreat in Agrippa's industrial park where ghouls could live without fear of harassment or bounty hunters.

To solve the problems of providing the ghouls' unsavory diet, Shepherd turned his attention toward the **Hammond Necroplex**, a vast, modern-day crypt and crematorium in even worse financial condition than Agrippa had been. The ghoul approached the director of the company with the proverbial offer he could not refuse: Shepherd would pay the necroplex director handsomely if he agreed to deposit bodies slated for entombment and/or cremation into the sewers beneath the city streets to feed Shepherd's ghouls. As an added inducement, Shepherd offered to refrain from publicizing certain sexually explicit simsense recordings that his hirelings had discovered. For a time, the arrangement worked well, until the ongoing desecration awakened a vengeful spirit in the necroplex. Three weeks ago, the angry spirit expressed its outrage by killing everyone on duty in the Hammond Necroplex facility except the director.

Shortly before the spirit went on its rampage in the necroplex, a quality control inspector named **Griffin Moore** in the employ of **Multitech International** spotted a serious flaw in the design of an optical chip intended for use in the MPCP of a new, military-grade cyberdeck. He reported the flaw to his superiors, who thanked him for his vigilance but informed him that they knew of the problem. Suspicious of their brusque brush-off with regard to such a crucial component, Griffin decided to do a little investigation on his own. Using stolen passcodes, the inspector slipped into the R&D lab and hacked into Multitech's design system, calling up the blueprints for the flawed chip. He discovered that the flaw was in fact a series of intentional shortcuts intended to reduce manufacturing time and thereby cut costs. However, the shortcuts would also render the final product virtually useless.

INTRODUCTION

Years ago, Griffin had replaced his rapidly failing right eye with a camera-rigged cybereye. Having discovered evidence of massive fraud by Multitech, Griffin used his cybereye to take digital photographs of every optical chip blueprint. The camera stored the incriminating images on an internal memory chip.

Unfortunately for the hapless Mr. Moore, his superiors had taken his report much more seriously than he realized. As he drove home from the lab with the evidence, a company thug ran Griffin's car off a cloverleaf. The employee of the month was pronounced dead on arrival at the nearest hospital, and after a tasteful memorial service in the Ecumenical Pavilion, was laid to rest in the Hammond Necroplex. Once the mourners had departed, the necroplex staff prepared the body as the director had instructed them to and deposited the butchered remains in the sewers beneath the complex. Griffin's body fed a family of four ghouls for a week; they made his inedible remains part of their nest, including his cybereye and the protected memory cavity embedded in the skull's eye socket.

Ten days after Griffin Moore's death, Lone Star picked up a couple of members of the **Iron Legion**, a notoriously violent street gang, for peddling black-market BTLs. To raise bail money, the gang organized a ghoul hunt. For years, the city of Seattle has maintained a bounty on ghouls, making them a popular and legal target for anyone with a gun. The Iron Legion has made a game of bagging ghouls, keeping score with gruesome tattoos. Following rumors rampant in the sprawl, these particular gangsters headed for the sewers and cut a bloody swath through the first ghoul enclave they found.

When the smoke cleared, the gang waded through the blood and shell casings in search of enough proof of ghoul killings to collect their bounty. As was their usual habit, they also took whatever salvage happened to be lying around. A Legionnaire named **Breaker** happened upon what was left of Griffin Moore's body and harvested his cybereye with a deft stroke of a penknife. Later that day, Breaker sold the eye to **Vanian**, a local fence specializing in cybertech. Vanian discovered the camera and retrieved a single image from its resident memory; intrigued by his find, he sent a copy of it to a friend named **Neil Scott** for analysis.

Upon hearing of the gang massacre, Shepherd sent his people to the sewers in search of survivors. One of Shepherd's technicians spotted the protected cavity in Griffin's half-eaten skull that housed the missing cybereye's internal memory. Prying the skull open with a crowbar, he retrieved the camera's memory chip. His analysis of it suggested the nature and origin of the blueprints, but without the plans for the final chip the data was virtually useless. The missing blueprint is the one that remained within the short-term memory in the actual cybereye, discovered by Breaker and passed to the fence Vanian.

Seeing an opportunity to exact revenge against the Iron Legion and to simultaneously acquire vast wealth and power with which to further his goals, Shepherd hired a notorious runner named **Clean Steve** to track the Iron Legion, find the missing blueprint and retrieve it by any means necessary, and then kill a gang member for every dead ghoul. Shepherd intends to use the complete set of optical blueprints, with their unsavory evidence of fraud, to blackmail Multitech into putting him on its board of directors. This position will make him one of the most powerful men in the city. As the runners enter the story, Clean Steve is already hot on the trail of the Iron Legion.

Meanwhile, Neil Scott deciphered the blueprint from Vanian. Realizing its significance and the danger that it represented, Neil decided to confront the optical chip's designer, hoping that the meeting might help him figure out how to stay alive. Unfortunately, the designer tipped off Multitech; Neil fell prey to a sniper on the way home from work. Before he died, however, Neil wrote a letter to his sister **Erin Scott**, also known as the shadowrunner **Alpha Blue,** containing a copy of the blueprint and his analysis. Upon hearing of Neil's death and receiving the letter, Erin swore to avenge his death by bringing Multitech to its knees. Unable to inflict enough damage going solo, Alpha Blue wants to hire an experienced team to help her out. . .

The runners must first figure out what the blueprint is and how it can be used to harm Multitech. In order to give Alpha Blue her revenge, they must obtain the rest of the evidence of Multitech's fraud—the complete set of chip blueprints copied by Griffin Moore. To find and acquire all the blueprints, the runners must tangle with the Iron Legion, hotshot assassin Clean Steve, and a powerful megacorp determined to stop them at any cost. Ultimately, the runners' investigation leads them to a final confrontation with Adam Shepherd and a veritable army of angry ghouls fighting for their own survival.

A GRAVE CONCERN

TELL IT TO THEM STRAIGHT

You've gone to meets in all kinds of exotic places in your day, but you never dreamed you'd talk biz in a corpse house. Death isn't something most runners care to be reminded of: it follows them too closely. One slip, and Joe Shadowrunner's dead meat. If not for your Johnson's reputation, you'd never have come to this dead zone: certainly not so quickly.

You circle around to the alley, picking your way over derelicts and around dumpsters in search of the back door. Two hired guns loiter by it, waiting to let you in—a couple of real bruisers. They look familiar; high-priced talent, unless you miss your guess. Someone seems uptight about security. Never a good sign, chummer. Never a good sign.

The inside depresses you even more than the outside, though you wouldn't have thought that was possible during your alley stroll. It's cleaner inside, but darker. A couple of caskets stand open on lintels; you firmly resist the morbid temptation to peek inside. One of the thugs leads you past the mourning gallery through the makeup room, where tomorrow's star attraction is receiving her final makeover. Plug 'em and plant 'em, that's how it goes. Here today, burned or buried tomorrow.

Lovely thought.

Your host awaits you in a back room filled with caskets, Remington Roomsweeper in hand but held in a relaxed pose. Your Mr. Johnson is a Ms., a dark-haired beauty in a form-fitting bodysuit of blue leather adorned with chrome studs and chains. The look on her face is one you've seen before, usually after a run gone bad. She's lost someone, and there'll be hell to pay as soon as she finds out where the accounting is due. As you enter, she dismisses the hired help with a wave. Once alone in the room with you, she sets the hardware down on the lid of a rosewood casket and starts her pitch...

HOOKS

Anger and grief charge every moment of this encounter. Erin Scott has just lost her brother, the only person in the world who really meant something to her, and she is dealing with her grief by focusing all of her considerable energy on avenging his murder. The sheer emotional impact of seeing this grieving beauty in the unsettling environment of a funeral parlor should shake the characters out of the average runner's knee-jerk cynicism long enough for Erin to deliver her pitch. Ideally, she evokes sympathy from the runners, giving them a stronger motivation for helping her than the mere prospect of fattening their credsticks. Also, play up the imagery associated with death: caskets, shrouds, guttering candles in darkened rooms, the sweetish smell of preservative chemicals, and so on. Use these images to set the stage for the rest of the adventure.

BEHIND THE SCENES

The introduction to this adventure assumes that the characters are looking for work, have heard about an emergency job from their usual fixer, and have chosen to make the rendezvous at the funeral parlor. If the gamemaster believes that the players or their characters might not play along, the adventure can begin from the fixer's initial contact.

If the player characters do not have a regular fixer, they will be approached by a mysterious, oriental fellow who tells them about a job and arranges a meeting with Alpha Blue. He insists on the funeral parlor, and remains adamant no matter how much the runners object.

The best way to ensure that the player characters take the job is to introduce Alpha Blue to them before running this adventure. As an experienced street samurai, she can be worked into virtually any scenario the gamemaster chooses, and the player characters can get to know her. When she asks her new friends for help at the beginning of this adventure, the player characters may well go to the mat for her in a way that they would not for a stranger.

A GRAVE CONCERN

SETTING THE STAGE

Throughout this encounter, the gamemaster should keep in mind the following background information. Depending on the questions that the player characters ask her, Alpha Blue may tell them some or all of it (see **Questions and Answers**, following).

The moment Neil Scott realized what the fence Vanian had sent him, he knew his life had gotten dirt cheap. Fearing that someone might take him out before he figured out his next move, he sent an electronic letter to his sister Erin, enclosing a copy of Vanian's business card and a copy of the blueprint. Erin, aka Alpha Blue, received the letter shortly after friends at Lone Star tipped her off to Neil's murder.

In the letter, Neil explained that Vanian hired him to analyze the blueprint, and that the print's designer had intentionally or unintentionally incorporated a defect to create a cheaper but inferior product. Neil also discovered that the designer of the blueprint was a man named Dutch Donovan, a hotshot currently employed by Multitech Corporation.

Erin believes that Multitech engineered her brother's death because he knew too much, and she wants revenge. If possible, she intends to prove publicly that the company's designers are cheating their customers. Unable to acquire that proof on her own, she needs the player characters to confirm her brother's suspicions and gather the necessary evidence. She is, of course, willing to pay handsomely for their services.

Her pitch, though simple, is unusual in the shadowrunning profession: Alpha Blue opts for total honesty. By playing it straight with the runners, she hopes to gain their trust. Though such honesty can make her vulnerable to an unscrupulous team, Alpha Blue needs reliable help fast if she wants any chance to avenge her brother's death. At any time, the hatchet boys who geeked Neil may learn of the letter he sent and come gunning for her. Her only hope for payback lies in getting a top-gun team of runners on her side to dig the skeletons out of Multitech's closet.

Once the runners reach the back room, the gamemaster may read the following aloud as a monologue or paraphrase it into a conversation:

"Thank you for coming. I know the surroundings are a little unusual, but I have my reasons for meeting you here. Any inconvenience I've put you to, I'll pay you for.

"Some of you may know me as Alpha Blue. Normally I work your side of the trade, but I have some personal biz that I can't handle myself. Off the streets, my name is Erin Scott. I tell you this because I need your trust and your help, and I don't have time for the usual games. You're pros—so am I. Here's hoping we can cut the drek and get to work.

"Last night, somebody shot my brother Neil in cold blood while he was on his way home from his downtown office. This morning I got a chunk of interesting mail that he sent me just prior to heading home."

At this point, Erin retrieves the letter, blueprint, and business card from a nearby shelf and passes them to one of the player characters. Give the players Handouts 1, 2 and 3 (pp. 70-71). Give the team a few minutes to peruse the contents, then continue with the following:

"I figure Multitech pulled the trigger. Neil said he found something incriminating in that blueprint, and he paid a high price for his insight. The fence who sent him that blueprint got it from somewhere. I want you to find out how Vanian got his mitts on the fragging thing and get me enough evidence to take the Multitech bastards down.

"I have a few friends in Lone Star who can pull strings to slow down the investigation into Neil's death. Hopefully, you can find what you need before the law gets wise. If not, you'll be dodging the badge at every turn. As long as the victim's not one of us shadowfolk, murder is still serious business in this part of town.

"I'd bet a thousand nuyen to a CAS dollar that Multitech is already rolling. Taking out Neil looks to me like the first step for the cleanup crew; if they're any good at their job, they'll be searching for every other possible leak so they can plug it. That means Vanian, chummers. If you want to talk to him, you'd better beat feet.

"I chose to meet with you because you jokers have a rep for good work and for slotting it when you have to. If you decide not to help me, then stay out of my way. One way or another, I will avenge Neil's death. Do we have a deal, or do I need to go elsewhere?"

QUESTIONS AND ANSWERS

Before committing themselves to the run, the team will probably want more information about the job. Alpha Blue has not had much time to do legwork, so her information is still pretty sketchy. However, she readily shares what little she knows about the blueprint, Neil and his death, Dutch Donovan, Multitech, and Vanian.

Blueprint

If the player characters ask what the blueprint is for, Blue says, "Neil said it was part of a flawed design for an optical chip, but he didn't say how Multitech planned to use it. I figure the rest of the design must be somewhere."

Dutch Donovan

If the runners ask about Dutch Donovan, Blue replies, "Apparently our chummer Dutch has quite a rep in corp circles. He's a chip designer, a real techno-geek; my brother thought a lot of his work. I remember hearing his name come up from time to time before this business started. He used to ride the cutting edge, but stopped making headlines about four or five years ago. I figured he was dead. Guess not."

Neil Scott

Erin was very close to her brother and gladly talks about him, but because she is still in mourning she tends to drift into reminiscences. The gamemaster should improvise anecdotes, at least one or two showing the two of them bailing each other out of trouble. Once Erin starts talking about their childhood, the runners may find it difficult to get her back on track, but they had best be tactful. At this stage of the game, their prospective employer could take any perceived slight extremely badly, and might even pull the run out from under them.

A GRAVE CONCERN

In addition to childhood memories, Erin can tell the runners that Neil worked freelance identifying and repairing black-market tech for scavengers like Vanian. Though he lacked formal education, he picked up enough knowledge of computers and cybertech on his own to build a reputation for reliability and discretion. Despite his connections in the shadows, Neil was basically a liner who worked the shady side because it gave him more freedom than a corp job to play with different pieces of tech.

If the runners ask Erin for additional information about Neil's murder, she tells them what she knows, but clearly finds it a painful subject. The runners may need to be patient while she gets the words out.

"I saw a copy of the initial report filed by the Lone Star badge assigned to the case. Never mind how. The report said Neil was on his way home from the downtown office where he does most of his work. A typical cybergeek, he was methodical to a fault: he drove the same route to work and back every day. Not even fear for his life could make him change; or maybe he figured they weren't onto him yet. Whatever the reason, he didn't change his route. When his Jackrabbit stopped for a red light at the intersection of Leopold and Loeb, a sniper opened fire. The bullets ripped through the car's cheap plastic body panels and into Neil's head and chest.

"Neither the coroner's report nor the ballistics analysis have come in yet, but I doubt the results can tell us anything we don't already know. Neil was DOA at Lewis Memorial—there's no doubt about the cause of death. Bystanders near the intersection reported seeing a man with a gun on a nearby rooftop, but so far Lone Star has yet to turn up anyone who got a good enough look at the gunman to make a positive ID. Considering the neighborhood, I doubt anyone will come forward. Nobody around those parts has much liking for the badge. That's all I know; do what you can with it."

Multitech

If the runners ask about Multitech, Alpha Blue's temper flares up. She believes the company killed her brother, and she hates them for it. She tells the runners the following:

"Multitech manufactures short runs of high-tech components for other companies. Their biggest customers include Henderson Multicom, Fuchi, and Magnuson, but they have dozens of other clients that they also work with on a regular basis. I haven't had time to do too much digging, and so far I haven't found anything worth telling; I'll let you know as soon as I do. Multitech's a dirty outfit, and I will bring them down."

Vanian

Erin has no idea what kind of relationship Vanian had with her brother, or what part (if any) he played in Neil's death. If the runners ask, she tells them the following:

"Don't know much about the fragger. I asked around a little when I got his card, but didn't have time to get the 411 from the street. He's a fence with a jones for tech, especially exotic cyberware. I hear he's a straight shooter, but you never know."

A GRAVE CONCERN

MAKING THE DEAL

Erin has earned meganuyen as Alpha Blue and intends to spare no expense in the pursuit of justice, but will not throw her money away. Years of running the shadows have made her a shrewd negotiator. The gamemaster determines the exact amount of her initial offer; ideally, he should make it high enough to tempt the runners but not high enough to bowl them over. To judge how much nuyen this run should net the runners, the gamemaster should take into account their lifestyles and expenses, as well as the type of game he wants to run. Does the gamemaster want the runners to scrape by, or to be secretly well-off? Should they need multiple jobs each month to meet their expenses, or only one? Once the gamemaster has chosen a base fee for the run, the runners should use standard negotiation procedures to drive the price higher.

If Alpha Blue's money seems inadequate, she may tell the runners that she takes their help as a personal favor and will gladly reciprocate. As a well-connected runner, she can do plenty for them. Even if they have no immediate need for a street samurai, she can perform other services for them. For example, Alpha Blue has several contacts in the black market who might be able to obtain exotic equipment for the runners at something of a discount.

Erin will do almost anything to hire the runners, because she has little time to waste. She is smart enough, however, not to show her desperation. If the runners stick to their guns they can negotiate excellent terms, but if they try to take too much advantage of their Johnson she will withdraw her offer and look elsewhere. On the other hand, if the runners seem sympathetic to her cause and keep their demands reasonable, Alpha Blue becomes their ally for life.

THE LADY VANISHES

If the team takes the job, Alpha Blue lets them know that they are pretty much on their own for the duration. Concerned for her own safety, she intends to disappear for awhile. She promises to check in on the runners from time to time, but cannot tell them when or how often.

Several times during the adventure, Blue should call in to see how the team is doing. If the player characters get into trouble or miss a vital clue, the gamemaster can use one of Alpha Blue's vidphone calls to get them back on track. The gamemaster should not overuse this device, however, or it may become a crutch that makes the actions of the runners irrelevant. As a rule of thumb, assume that she can only help the runners out once. If the team hoses up more than once, they have to get themselves out of drek.

GETTING DOWN TO BIZ

Once the player characters agree to take the run, Erin summarizes their options.

Read the following aloud to the players, or paraphrase it:

"You'd best get moving. I figured Lone Star would start their investigation at Neil's apartment, so I cleaned it out on my way here. Stay well clear of the place; it'll be crawling with cops. Nothing to find there, anyway; I made sure of that. You might try checking out the scene of the crime at Leopold & Loeb, but hold off on that for an hour or two. That'll give Lone Star time to finish doing whatever the frag they do.

"Neil's lab is your best bet. His office is downtown, in an industrial complex by the name of Gibson Hall. I'll get you the exact address and his passcard. If you go there, I would appreciate your picking up anything that looks like Neil's personal effects and bringing them to me.

"You'll also want to check on Vanian, fast. You have his business address on his card; I don't know where he dosses down. I also have a home address for Dutch Donovan, and for the Multitech branch office where he works. I wish you luck; you may need it."

At this point, the runners have several options. Cautious runners might want to start with a little legwork, but sooner or later they will have to hit the streets. If the runners take Erin's advice and start their investigation at Neil's lab, go to **Home Away From Home**, p. 13. If they start at the murder site, go to **Scene of the Crime**, p. 26. If they turn up at Vanian's storefront, go to **Vanian's Place**, p. 19. If they decide to look for Donovan at his home, go to **Welcome to my Parlor**, p. 22; if they decide to take on Multitech directly, go to **Lion's Den**, p. 38.

DEBUGGING

Not much can go wrong at this point, aside from the usual problems that can surface with any employer. The runners may decide initially not to take the job; if this happens, Alpha Blue can take a few steps to ensure their cooperation. For example, most shadowrunners have past secrets that they prefer to keep buried; Alpha Blue has the resources to find out the runners' deep darks, and is not above threatening blackmail to get what she wants. Of course, this hardball tactic may well galvanize the runners' resistance to her offer, putting them at odds with a tough, determined street samurai. The gamemaster may wish to point out that fact if the players seem reluctant.

In the unlikely but unfortunate instance that the runners absolutely refuse to work for Erin Scott, they may receive a similar offer of employment from the ghoul business magnate, Adam Shepherd. If necessary, the gamemaster may use this device as a last resort to bring the runners into the adventure. Shepherd cares nothing for Neil Scott, of course; he only wants the blueprint to further his own blackmail scheme, and so the gamemaster must rethink a few of the encounters. The objectives remain similar enough, however, that the adventure can still work from the ghoul's point of view.

HOME AWAY FROM HOME

TELL IT TO THEM STRAIGHT

Gibson Hall turns out to be a high-rise in an industrial park slowly going to seed. The high-rise leases office space to anyone with enough nuyen to pay six months' rent up front. From what Alpha Blue told you, Neil maintained a small office on the second floor where he could work in peace.

You sleaze past the bored-looking guard at the security desk without a glitch, then take a short ride in a glass elevator up the central shaft. On the second floor, you jander down the hall to room 213. Cracking the simple identicard system that keeps the office off-limits to outsiders like you might have posed a time-consuming inconvenience, but Alpha Blue was one step ahead of the game. You swipe the duplicate card she gave you down the slot; the door lock clicks open, and you step inside.

As you enter, the overhead lights flicker to life and a synthesized voice asks if everything is all right. It wants to know why you're late. It sounds concerned, like a doting mother, and you feel a moment's pity for Neil Scott. Night after night the poor slot came to this sterile, cramped office to stare at a bank of computer screens for hours on end, his only company a primitive faux-personality system. Neil Scott must have been a lonely man until a high-velocity slug put him out of his misery.

HOOKS

Play up the sense of discomfort, bordering on embarrassment. After their encounter with Erin Scott, the runners should feel awkward sifting through the inanimate remnants of her brother's life. Walking around Neil's lab should make them feel as if they are walking around his tomb. Describe the dead man's personal effects; he might have the picture of a simsense starlet hidden in his desk drawer, or some memento of a long-ago triumph such as a third-grade spelling medal. Many of Neil's personal items should reflect his lonely existence, painting a picture of a man with little in his life save work, memories, and fantasies.

HOME AWAY FROM HOME

BEHIND THE SCENES

When Multitech activated its cleanup crew, they paid a prompt visit to Neil Scott's lab. After efficiently and thoroughly searching the premises, they rigged a time bomb powerful enough to wipe out half the second floor in an effort to destroy any evidence of their presence that they might have left behind (see **Finding the Bomb**, following).

The gamemaster should give the player characters a chance to search most of the lab before introducing the bomb threat. If they move quickly, they can find a few clues to the mystery of Neil's murder.

Not exactly a high-security facility, Gibson Hall poses little challenge to the runners in terms of getting in. The building has a central security office, as well as a guard station in the lobby. The guards are poorly paid and out of practice: they do the minimum required of them, but no more. As long as the team does not come rolling in armed to the teeth, they should attract little attention.

SECURITY GUARDS (8)

B	Q	S	I	C	W	E	R	Armor
3	3	3	2	2	2	6	2	2/1

Initiative: 2 + 1D6
Threat/Professional Rating: 2/2
Skills: Etiquette (Corporate) 2, Firearms 3
Gear: Ares Predator [Heavy Pistol, 15 (clip), SA, 9M, w/2 extra clips], Armor Vest (2/1), Plastic Restraints

Far from the cream of the crop, these part-timers serve as little more than a deterrent for the easily intimidated. They strut around in their smart, blue uniforms trying to impress the secretaries, but are virtually useless when the lead starts to fly. After hours, they patrol in pairs and have orders to radio in anything suspicious to the central office.

The gamemaster may also want to create a few items for the runners to return to Erin. These things should serve as poignant reminders of his closeness to his sister: a photo of them as children hugging each other, a long-ago birthday card, and so on. Push plenty of buttons; make the runners feel the pain.

HOME AWAY FROM HOME

GIBSON HALL COMPUTER SYSTEM

Even though Alpha Blue gave them Neil's passcard, the runners may decide to break into his lab through the Matrix, particularly if the team includes a decker who habitually scouts ahead before the rest of the team starts the run. In this particular case, a Matrix run is a mistake. Because of the sensitive nature of his work, Neil seldom used the public nodes, preferring a small, separate mainframe of his own design. This mainframe is not connected to the Matrix. All other systems in the building, however, are connected to both the Matrix and each other.

Every floor has its own subprocessor, connected to all of the equipment in the labs on that level. Each subprocessor, in turn, is linked to the Matrix. Any intrusion is likely to trigger an alert in several systems. The Gibson Hall System uses the UMS (Universal Matrix Specifications) image set: all of its constructs consist of interlocking geometric designs. If a decker triggers an active alert, the entire system shuts down within three Combat Turns.

SECURITY CHIEF

B	Q	S	C	I	W	E	R	Armor
4	5	4	4	3	5	6	4	4/3

Initiative: 4 + 1D6
Threat/Professional Rating: 4/3
Skills: Armed Combat 3, Etiquette (Corporate) 4, Firearms 4, Interrogation 3, Leadership 3, Unarmed Combat 3
Gear: Ares Predator [Heavy Pistol, 15 (clip), SA, 9M, w/2 extra clips, Laser Sight (−1 modifier to target numbers)], Armored Vest w/Plates (4/3)

A former cop, Jack Stone entered the field of private security looking for a regular paycheck with as little risk as possible. Most of the time, he gets exactly that; depending on how they handle themselves, however, the runners may put a definite cramp in his retirement plans. A bit more talented than his troops, Stone may pose something of a threat to the runners.

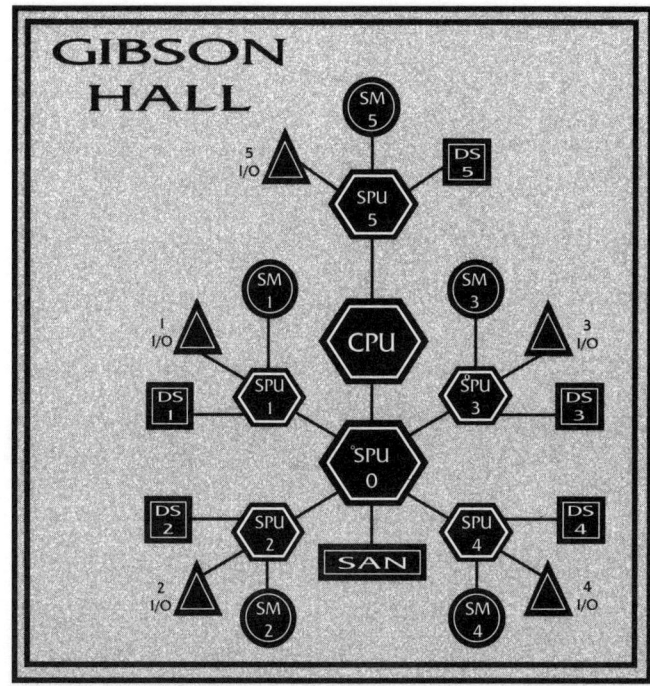

CPU = Central Processing Unit
DS = Datastore
I/OP = Input/Output Port
SAN = System Access Node
SM = Slave Module
SPU = Subprocessor Unit

SAN: Orange-4, Access 6.
SPU-0: Orange-6, Access 7, Trace and Report 7. This subprocessor protects the rest of the system from unwanted intrusion through the SAN and serves as a data junction that regulates traffic between the subprocessors and the CPU.
SPU-1: Orange-4, Access 5, Trace and Report 6. This subprocessing unit handles all traffic for the laboratories on the first floor.
    DS-1: Orange-5, Access 5.
    I/OP-1: Orange-5, Access 5.
    SM-1: Orange-5, Access 5.

CONDITION MONITOR

	LIGHT STUN	MODERATE STUN	SERIOUS STUN		DEADLY STUN
STUN	+1 TN# -1 Init.	+2 TN# -2 Init.	+3 TN# -3 Init.		Unc.
PHYSICAL	+1 TN# -1 Init.	+2 TN# -2 Init.	+3 TN# -3 Init.		Unc. maybe dead
	LIGHT WOUND	MODERATE WOUND	SERIOUS WOUND		DEADLY WOUND

HOME AWAY FROM HOME

SPU-2: Orange-4, Access 5, Trace and Report 6. This subprocessing unit handles all traffic for the laboratories on the second floor.

DS-2: Orange-5, Access 5. File locations for Room 213 exist in this datastore. If the team decker takes the time to examine the contents, he discovers that they are dummy files full of duplicates intended to make it look as though Neil was using the Gibson Hall System.

I/OP-2: Orange-5, Access 5. One of the terminals in Room 213 is connected to this port, but Neil seldom used it except to communicate with the building's landlord.

SM-2: Orange-5, Access 5. None of the equipment in Room 213 is connected to this module.

SPU-3: Orange-4, Access 5, Trace and Report 6. This subprocessing unit handles all of the traffic for the laboratories on the third floor.

DS-3: Orange-5, Access 5.

I/OP-3: Orange-5, Access 5.

SM-3: Orange-5, Access 5.

SPU-4: Orange-4, Access 5, Trace and Report 6. This subprocessing unit handles all of the traffic for the laboratories on the fourth floor.

DS-4: Orange-5, Access 5.

I/OP-4: Orange-5, Access 5.

SM-4: Orange-5, Access 5.

CPU: Red-6, Access 7, Trace and Burn 8. The system is designed so that nothing runs directly from the central processor. Instead, the subprocessing units on each floor handle all the system traffic.

SPU-5: Orange-6, Access 7, Tar Pit 7. This subprocessor is dedicated to security.

DS-5: Orange-5, Access 6, Trace and Report 6.

I/OP-5: Orange-5, Access 6, Trace and Report 6.

SM-5: Orange-5, Access 6, Trace and Report 6.

NEIL'S COMPUTER SYSTEM

Fortunately for the runners, it is possible to break into Neil's isolated system. The isolated system functions as a mini-matrix, whose architecture consists of the nodes that compose Neil's system. If a decker triggers an active alert, the entire system shuts down within three Combat Turns.

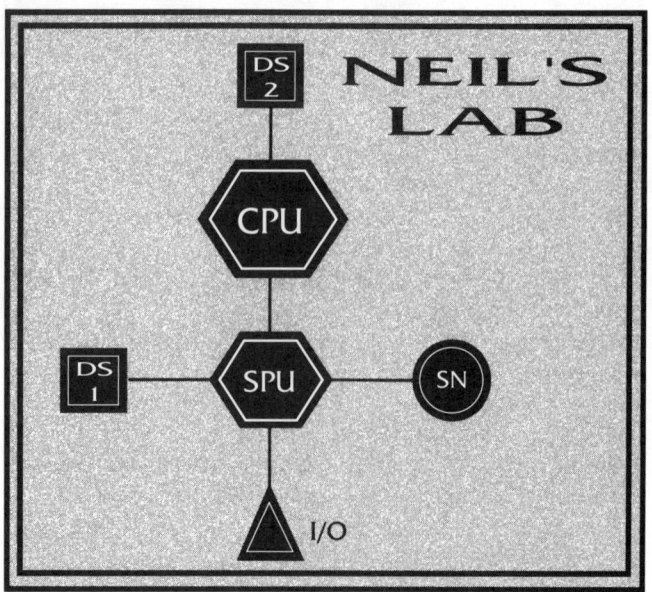

CPU = Central Processing Unit
DS = Datastore
I/OP = Input/Output Port
SM = Slave Module
SPU = Subprocessor Unit

SPU: Orange-4, Access 5, Trace and Report 6.

DS-1: Orange-5, Access 5. Neil used this datastore as a data dump, storing nothing of real importance in it.

I/OP: Orange-5, Access 5. Three terminals are connected to the mainframe via this port, and also to several datascreens inside the room.

SM: Orange-5, Access 5. This module controls all of the testing equipment in Neil's lab.

CPU: Red-6, Access 7, Trace and Burn 8.

DS-2: Orange-5, Access 6, Trace and Report 6. If the runners break into this secure datastore, named "current projects," they gain access to the following files and can read, copy, or print them.

BP Botch Bypass

This file contains half a dozen versions of a netrunning program. To determine the nature of the program, the team decker or other runner must make a Computer (5) Test. If he achieves at least 1 success, he recognizes the program as an incomplete attack program of some kind. If he achieves 2 successes, he realizes that the program is so simple that it hardly seems worth bothering to construct. If he achieves 3 or more successes, he realizes that the program is designed to attack a specific flaw in the target's MPCP program, and that it only works if the flaw is present. The decker cannot tell what that flaw is, because Neil did not know for certain either.

Later on in the adventure, the runners may obtain the rest of the Multitech optical chip blueprints. If they do, a player character with Computer Skill can use the data in them to finish Neil's attack program, giving the runners a powerful weapon against any MPCP that employs the flawed Multitech chips. If the gamemaster wants to pursue this particular plot line, he must determine how difficult the runner with Computer Skill finds his or her task.

BP Comp/Sorted Prints

This file contains close to a hundred blueprints. A decker or other runner who achieves at least 1 success on a Computer (6) Test recognizes them as optical chip designs. If he achieves 3 or more successes, he recognizes the chips as those used in master persona control programs. Most of the prints in this file are declassified documents pertaining to obsolete models made by various companies, but 20 megapulses worth of prints are recent designs worth quite a bit on the black market. The exact value of these blueprints is up to the gamemaster.

Storm Front TD

This file contains 10 mp of technical data on a weather survey satellite, and has nothing to do with the Multitech blueprints. Designs for a few optical chips to be used in the satellite's CPU may mislead runners overanxious to make a connection between Multitech and anything they find in Neil's lab. The runners might find a buyer for the data, but only after considerable looking.

16 EYE WITNESS

HOME AWAY FROM HOME

LAB LAYOUT

The layout and accouterments of Neil's workshop reflect his economical lifestyle. He had few friends, and spent most of his time alone in his lab. To give himself company, he created a simple personality program capable of carrying on rudimentary conversation. The program, which he named Jimmy, has only a short-term memory and tends to repeat itself. It has no access to the computer's datastore. As the runners search the lab, Jimmy keeps up a constant stream of meaningless chatter.

At some time during their search, either before or after the runners discover the bomb left by Multitech's thugs, one of them should realize that the lab has been professionally searched prior to their arrival. Nothing seems out of place, yet it should seem obvious to the other player characters once one of them points it out. Once they discover the bomb, of course, they know for certain that someone has beaten them to the punch.

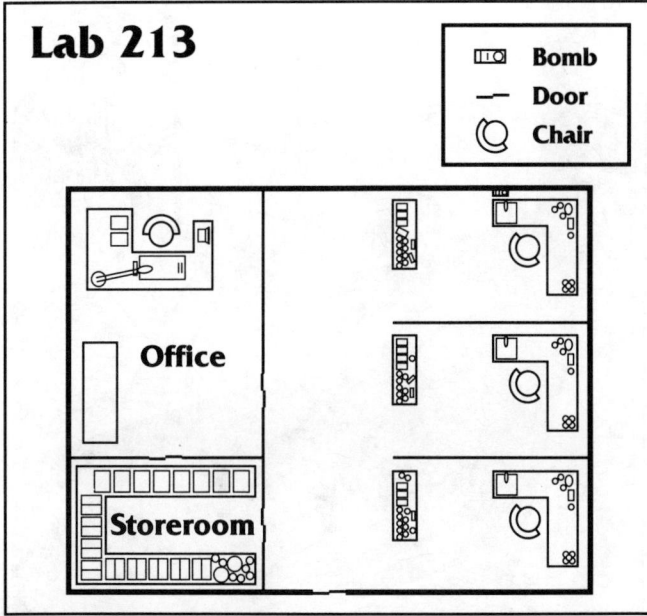

Lab

The lab has three work stations in its central area, all of which Neil used for various purposes. On a shelf in one of the stations is a Fuchi Cyber-4 deck and a small, wooden box containing the following program chips: Attack 2, Attack 3, a one-shot Attack 4, Slow 3, Medic 4, Shield 4, Analyze 3, Analyze 4, Browse 5, Decrypt 4, Deception 3, Deception 4 and a one-shot Sleaze 5. Each of the chips is in a black case with Neil's initials scratched on it.

Office

The office contains an impossibly neat desk with a few personal effects on it, a chair, and an almost-empty filing cabinet. Because of the clandestine nature of most of his projects, Neil never kept records of his business transactions. The runners find no contracts on file, and no addresses in the rolodex. In the top right-hand desk drawer is a credstick with a balance of 2,500 nuyen, a light pistol obviously never used or even cared for properly, and a still-sealed box of ammunition.

Storeroom

The shelves in the storeroom contain reams of paper, extra diskettes, cleaning supplies, and so on. One of the storage cabinets has a false back, behind which Neil stored his projects. In this secret compartment, the runners can find the three pieces of cybergear described below. In each case, the gamemaster decides how well the gear works and what price it might fetch.

The first item is a remote-firing mechanism, a palm-sized device that looks like a smartgun link with a booster and a high-gain antenna. The mechanism allows the user to trigger a fixed weapon at a range of up to 0.4 kilometers (a quarter of a mile).

The second item, a prototype cyberware scanner, is a portable device with a holographic screen that resembles a bug scanner. This item detects and identifies cybernetic enhancements at a range of up to 100 feet. The software, however, was never perfected, and so it works only intermittently when more than 10 feet from its target. It usually detects the presence and general type of cyberware, but has trouble making a specific, positive identification.

The third item, a battered Allegiance Alpha cyberdeck held together with duct tape, has prototype boards and optical cables sprouting out of it like weeds. The deck is rigged with redundant subprocessors that increase its load speed to 15. It should be clear to any decker that the principles behind the increased load speed might be adapted for a more agile deck such as a Fuchi, making this find potentially valuable for the runners at first glance. Jury-rigging such a deck, however, might prove difficult and would cost at least 15,000 nuyen. The deck should also include an uncorrectable flaw of the gamemaster's choice. For example, a player character might be required to roll 2D6 every time he or she loads a program at the increased rate: on a result of 10 or lower, the program is corrupted and unusable.

FINDING THE BOMB

As they search the lab and office, the runners should have no trouble finding the bomb planted by Multitech's goon squad. The size of a cigar box, the charge has been taped to a wall somewhere in Room 213. Unknown to the runners, there is a gas line behind the plastiboard. The small explosive charge, going off right by the gas line, will destroy much of the second floor when it blows.

Upon examination, the runners discover that the bomb has a timed fuse and a motion sensor that will set it off if they tamper with it. The timer has twenty minutes left on it, allowing the team plenty of time to get out of the building before it goes off. It should be clear to the runners that the bomb is not part of the lab's security system, but is instead a plant designed to demolish the lab.

To disarm the bomb without disturbing the motion sensor, a player must roll 3 or more successes in a Demolitions (6) Test. If the test is unsuccessful, the bomb will go off in the player character's face. If the runners fail to disarm the bomb or leave without disarming it, the nasty little package wipes out most of the second floor when it detonates. Unless disarmed, the bomb explodes with a 20D blast, reduced by 1 for every one-half meter the blast travels. Even taking that reduction into account, the bomb's placement ensures that it will bring down the ceiling and much of the adjoining structure.

HOME AWAY FROM HOME

The runners must decide what to do about the bomb. If they choose to, they may simply walk out: after all, Alpha Blue did not hire them to protect a bunch of labcoats in Gibson Hall. Walking out, however, demonstrates a certain callousness on the runners' part, and therefore the gamemaster may want to adjust Karma awards based on the team's actions in this encounter. They may get a few extra points for risking their own lives to disarm the bomb.

Clearing the Decks

If the player characters lack the skills to successfully disarm the bomb but still want to try to save some people, they have enough time to make a quick circuit of the second floor. Fortunately, not many people are around; the only other person in danger from the blast is an independent researcher named Leary, who leases the lab adjacent to Neil's. When the runners tell him he has to get out, he initially refuses because he is unwilling to abandon his equipment. If they convince him that the bomb threat is real, Leary begs the runners to help him evacuate key apparatus from his lab.

If the player characters save Leary's lab, they earn his gratitude and have made a potentially valuable contact whose skills may prove useful in future adventures. In this adventure, however, Leary can do little for the team. He knew Neil in passing; they had lunch a couple of times, but for the most part Neil kept to himself.

Leary

B	Q	S	C	I	W	E	R
5	2	4	4	6	5	4	4

CONDITION MONITOR				
	LIGHT STUN	MODERATE STUN	SERIOUS STUN	DEADLY STUN
STUN	+1 TN# / -1 Init.	+2 TN# / -2 Init.	+3 TN# / -3 Init.	Unc.
PHYSICAL	+1 TN# / -1 Init.	+2 TN# / -2 Init.	+3 TN# / -3 Init.	Unc. maybe dead
	LIGHT WOUND	MODERATE WOUND	SERIOUS WOUND	DEADLY WOUND

Initiative: 4 + 1D6
Threat/Professional Rating: 2/2
Skills: Biology 5, Biotech 7, Computer 6, Computer Theory 5, Cybertechnology 8, Electronics 7, Firearms 3, Physical Sciences 4, Unarmed Combat 3
Cyberware: Chipjack, Datajack, Datasoft Link, Display Link, 150 Mp of Memory

Thrown out of several universities and discharged from three respectable corporations for his radical ideas, Leary has decided to go it alone. Using his savings as investment capital, he is developing a device that interacts with organic memory in the same way that computers interact with conventional data. If it works, Leary can use his device to create specialized browse programs to search the subconscious for facts not accessible to conscious memory.

DEBUGGING

The little information still available in the lab is not critical to the adventure, so little can go wrong unless the runners get killed by the bomb. If the bomb destroys Neil's work, the runners will lose a few of the clues that might help them figure out the adventure background, but the lack of this information should not slow them down much. Their only objective in this encounter is survival.

If the runners have not already investigated Vanian the fence, his storefront is their next logical stop. Go to **Vanian's Place**, p. 19. If the runners feel that they have enough of an edge on either Dutch Donovan or Multitech, go to **Welcome to my Parlor** (p. 22) or **Lion's Den** (p. 38). Either of these choices should bring the adventure to a quick and bloody climax.

VANIAN'S PLACE

TELL IT TO THEM STRAIGHT

Alpha Blue gave you Vanian's address, in exactly the nasty part of town where you'd have expected to find it. Third gutter to the left and straight on 'til morning. Not exactly a prime location. Still, for a fence this Vanian character has guts. Few in his profession have the cojones to maintain a storefront; most fences don't care to advertise. Either Vanian's a real drekhead, or he has reason to be cocky. Wedged between a butcher shop that looks like nirvana for six-legged livestock and an all-night erotisense parlor, Vanian's reminds you of a perfectly legal, if unsavory, pawn shop.

HOOKS

The smell of cordite hangs heavy in the air. This encounter is intended to give the runners a healthy respect for the Multitech cleanup team; play up the effectiveness of Vanian's security system and the quick, clean execution of the two dead assistants the player characters find. Clearly, the search of Vanian's shop was conducted by professionals.

BEHIND THE SCENES

"Rat" Vanian is a well-known fence who conducts his business out of a small storefront. Unfortunately for the player characters, the Multitech cleanup crew arrived before they did and searched the shop quickly and efficiently, killing Vanian's two assistants in the process.

STOREFRONT SECURITY AND LAYOUT

Though its shabby appearance suggests otherwise, Vanian equipped his shop with an expensive security system. On closer examination, the runners discover that the front windows are reinforced with fiber-plastic weave composite and the front door is heavy-gauge steel. A person or persons unknown has disarmed the sophisticated keypad entry system. As soon as the runners reach the door, they realize that someone beat them to the shop.

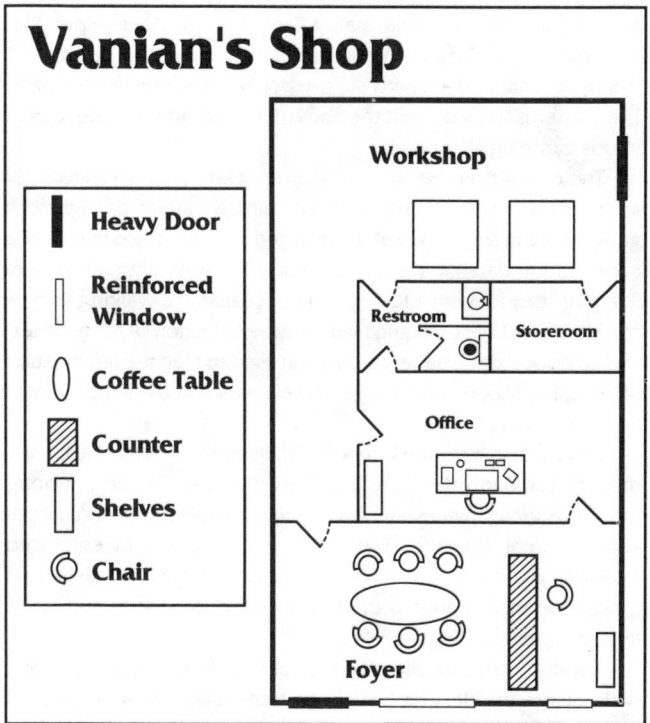

Foyer (A)

This waiting area encompasses a coffee table, several chairs, and a shelving unit, as well as a long counter. On the underside of the counter is a large button that sounds a silent alarm in the office and workshop. An Ares Predator lies on a small, hidden shelf suspended beneath the counter.

VANIAN'S PLACE

Office (B)

Vanian spends so much of his time at the shop that he installed a cot in the office for the odd moment when he needs to catnap. The office also includes a wall-size viewscreen for whiling away the hours between appointments, and a small table with a couple of chairs for business meetings. A dead man lies sprawled on the floor by the cot, his blood staining the area rug. On further examination, the runners discover that he is an oriental gentleman, shot three times in the chest with a high-caliber weapon.

Workshop (C)

In this large, back room Vanian cares for the gear that is his stock in trade. The walls are lined with shelves full of gear, and various bits and pieces lie scattered across the two work tables and the small desk. The wildly strewn components and papers give mute evidence of a struggle. Under one of the tables lies the corpse of a middle-aged technician, his chest ripped to shreds by a huge weapon loaded with explosive ammunition.

Storeroom (D)

If the runners decide to rob Vanian blind, they stand to make a tidy profit. They can easily resell or keep for themselves any amount of useful gear from the storeroom.

Against the left wall stands a weapons locker with a Maglock (3) and a Barrier Rating of 8. If the runners succeed in opening the cabinet, they find Vanian's stock of firearms: an Ares Predator, a Remington Roomsweeper, an AK-97 submachine gun, an AK-97 assault rifle, and a chrome-plated Ranger Arms SM-3 sniper rifle. Accessories include a Gas Vent II, a deluxe gyro mount, an external smartgun link, and a sound suppresser in a genuine leather case. The gamemaster may edit the above list of weapons as he sees fit for his campaign.

The cabinet on the right wall, also locked with a Maglock (3) and with a Barrier Rating of 8, contains a variety of high-tech gadgets including a slightly damaged micro-camcorder and a combination dataline tap and codebreaker, both with a Rating of 3; a bug scanner with a Rating of 1 concealed in a walking stick; a couple of pocket secretaries with a wide selection of accessories; and an optical data reader that Vanian used to read the information off of Griffin Moore's cybereye. The eye is not in the shop; Vanian has it with him.

Salvaged cyberware litters the shelves against the back wall, most of it so badly damaged that it is only good for parts. Among the more intact pieces are two complete right cyberarms, both with minimal damage. The first has two levels of enhanced strength, and the second has a compartment large enough to hold a small weapon. Vanian's cyberware collection also includes the following exotic items.

The first item is a collection of three plastic manacles and a belt with a large buckle. The buckle is a transmitter, its antenna built into the belt. The manacles are anklets that operate like squealers with bite: if someone wearing one of the manacles approaches within 100 yards of the active transmitter, a bundle of plastique concealed in the manacle explodes.

The second item is a footlocker, containing a motorcycle's rearview mirror and a machine gun. This experimental system, designed for use with a Yamaha Rapier, allows the rider to rear-fire the machine gun at pursuers using a smartgun link built into the rearview mirror. The distance between the mirror and the rider's eyes causes a slight problem that the system's designers have yet to overcome, so in game terms it gives no bonus.

The third item is an intricately carved, silk-lined wooden box containing a black pistol with a pearl handle, a matching silencer, and five rounds of ammunition. In game terms, this handmade weapon has the same statistics as an Ares Viper Slivergun. Though the gun is valuable, a smart player character will leave it be. If any runner makes an Etiquette (Street) (5) Test and rolls at least 2 successes, he or she recognizes yakuza symbols in the design on the box.

Restroom (E)

This room is an ordinary bathroom with three stalls, all of which are empty.

VANIAN'S ADDRESS

The dead bodies and the mess in the workshop let the player characters know that Vanian's has been searched. By sheer luck, however, the runners stumble upon a vital clue: Vanian's home address. The gamemaster should have all the player characters make Perception Tests against the secret target number of his choice, and tell the following to the runner who gets the closest result:

"As you carefully shift a box, you notice the edge of a piece of paper stuck to the bottom of it. Pulling it free, you find yourself holding a small envelope. Somebody sent this Vanian mope a paper letter, of all things. You turn it over and read the address on the front: Jack Vanian, 9280 Shady Hill Lane, Apt. # 2112, Redmond, Seattle, UCAS."

The address is Vanian's home. At this point, the player characters cannot tell if Multitech found it as well. (As it happens, they haven't, but they will shortly. That means that the cleanup crew will arrive at Vanian's home just after the runners do. Tough drek, chummers.)

If any of the more technically oriented runners examines the shop's security system, they find that it has a Matrix feeder set to transmit video signals to another location. The feeder connection is broken, most likely at the command of the signals' receiver. Though the runners cannot determine the receiver's location, the signals went to Vanian's home. The fence saw the whole shooting match go down at his shop, and wisely stayed in hiding (see **Rat's Nest**, p. 29).

A NEW PLAYER

The runners are not the only ones investigating the Multitech affair. Adam Shepherd/Eric Steward, the ghoul multimillionaire, hired his own team to find the missing blueprint upon obtaining the rest of the prints from Griffin Moore's corpse in the sewers (see **Plot Synopsis**, p. 7). Notorious runner Clean Steve and his hired guns close in on Vanian's shop just as the runners are getting ready to leave.

Clean Steve's entourage consists of four mercenary soldiers and four snipers. Keeping his mercs with him at all times, Steve positions the snipers on nearby rooftops. Despite the firepower backing him up, Clean Steve prefers to confront the player characters without resorting to combat. He tries to get as much information as possible from them without giving anything away about himself or his employer, and will try to set up a meeting at Club Nosferatu (see **Early Halloween**, p. 53) once he realizes that he can learn no more in this intimidating setting. Statistics for the mercs and snipers appear below; for Clean Steve's game statistics, see **Cast of Shadows**, p. 67.

Mercenaries (4)

B	Q	S	C	I	W	E	R	Armor
5	5	4	2	3	4	3	4 (8)	5/3

Initiative: 8 + 3D6
Threat/Professional Rating: 5/3
Skills: Armed Combat 4, Etiquette (Street) 4, Firearms 5, Unarmed Combat 4
Cyberware: Wired Reflexes (2)
Gear: Ares Predator [Heavy Pistol, 15 (clip), SA, 9M, w/2 extra clips and Laser Sight (–1 modifier to target numbers)], Armor Jacket (5/3), Club [Reach 1, 6M Stun], Heckler & Koch HK227 [SMG, 28 (clip) SA/BF/FA, 7M, w/2 extra clips, Gas Vent II]

Snipers (4)

B	Q	S	C	I	W	E	R	Armor
4	6	4	5	4	4	6	5	2/1

Initiative: 5 + 1D6
Threat/Professional Rating: 4/3
Skills: Armed Combat 3, Etiquette (Street) 4, Firearms 6, Unarmed Combat 3
Gear: Armor Vest (2/1), Heckler & Koch HK227 [SMG, 28 (clip) SA/BF/FA, 7M, w/3 extra clips, Gas Vent II]

Throughout this encounter, Steve plays it cool and straight. He wants to know who the runners are working for, and what (if anything) they have found in the shop. More than likely, they will refuse to tell him much. At this point he may get annoyed, but will choose not to beat out of them whatever he thinks they may know. Instead, he will let them know that he can be reached through Caine, the owner of Club Nosferatu (see **Early Halloween**, p. 53).

Clean Steve will recognize one of the runners, and vice versa. This mutual recognition sets up a channel of communication between Clean Steve and the runners, to be used later in the adventure. If the runners wish to do legwork on Clean Steve at this point, go to **Legwork**, p. 60. More likely, the runners will want to track down Vanian. If so, go to **Rat's Nest**, p. 29. They may also choose to investigate Dutch Donovan (**Welcome to my Parlor**, p. 22), or the scene of Neil's murder (**Scene of the Crime**, p. 26).

DEBUGGING

The player characters should have realized by now that time is of the essence in this adventure. If the runners choose to wait around and watch the shop, Steve and his crew will come and go; no one else will appear until another of Vanian's assistants arrives shortly after sunrise to open up. Meanwhile, of course, Multitech's hired guns are getting closer to their goal and eliminating the runners' potential avenues of investigation.

When Vanian's assistant discovers the dead bodies, he locks up the place, calls Lone Star, and waits until help arrives. He snatches the Predator from under the counter and hides in the storeroom until he hears sirens. If the runners choose to follow him in, they will face a firefight. No matter what, they should not loiter too long; Vanian made regular "donations" to the local Lone Star stationhouse, so two cruisers will arrive in short order. The presence of Seattle's finest could make things very awkward for the runners.

EYE WITNESS

WELCOME TO MY PARLOR

TELL IT TO THEM STRAIGHT

You vaguely remember hearing stories about Dutch Donovan. Not so many years ago, he was ace on the shady side of the street. Must have been tough to leave the good life behind for a prefab duplex in the 'burbs. Everything about this place reeks of the mainstream: the synthturf, the uniform hedgerows and identical trees, and the neat little rows of whitewashed buildings. They might as well put signs over every door that read, "Home of Corporate Wageslave" in huge, neon letters. Welcome to the suburban nightmare, chummers.

HOOKS

This encounter should take the runners completely by surprise. Nothing in the immediate environment warns them about the coming ambush. When the attack comes, increase the pressure by speeding up the combat, having the players make dice rolls faster and forcing snap decisions to keep them off balance.

BEHIND THE SCENES

Dutch Donovan's lucrative and exclusive contract with Multitech includes a house in Smallville, a suburban housing development wholly owned by the company and its subsidiaries. Almost all of the tenants are employees of Multitech.

When Neil Scott approached Dutch with the stolen blueprint, the designer played company stooge and reported the incident to his superiors. For his loyalty, he received the reward of an immediate transfer to Multitech's Shanghai office. The top execs might have preferred to ventilate him along with Neil just to make things extra tidy, but as one of the top talents in his field Dutch remains too valuable a resource to sacrifice. Multitech has stationed a team of troubleshooters in the Smallville complex ever since Neil Scott's murder, in case anyone came looking for Dutch. The runners' arrival plays directly into the enemy's hands. Though the runners do not realize it, Multitech has turned the whole complex into a trap from which they may never escape.

DONOVAN'S PLACE

Dutch left his Smallville digs several days ago. As soon as he spilled the data about the stolen chip print, the company troubleshooters helped him pack and hustled him onto a corporate jet bound for Shanghai, then descended on his apartment. They replaced enough of his personal effects to give the place a lived-in look, and even stationed someone inside the house to pose as the designer for the benefit of observers.

Dutch Donovan/Troubleshooter

B	Q	S	C	I	W	E	R	Armor
5	6	5	4	4	6	2.1	5 (9)	5/3

Initiative: 9 + 3D6
Threat/Professional Rating: 4/4
Skills: Armed Combat 3, Athletics 4, Etiquette (Corporate) 3, Firearms 5, Stealth (Urban) 4, Throwing Weapons (Non-Aerodynamic) 3, Unarmed Combat 4
Cyberware: Cybereyes, Low-Light w/Flare Compensation; Retractable Hand Razors, Smartlink, Wired Reflexes (2)
Gear: Ares Predator [Heavy Pistol, 15 (clip), SA, 9M, w/2 extra clips and Laser Sight (–1 modifier to target numbers)], Armor Jacket (5/3), Heckler & Koch HK227 [SMG, 28 (clip) SA/BF/FA, 7M, w/2 extra clips, Gas Vent II]

The Multitech troubleshooter posing as Donovan is one of the company's best operatives. The voice modulator he wears

allows him to simulate the designer's voice, but he had no time to craft a decent false face. He stays inside the house, well out of sight. He questions any visitors at length, trying to get as much information as he can before setting the ambush in motion. Before they blow anyone away, Multitech wants badly to know who might have the blueprints. A competitor could gain valuable information from them, or use them against Multitech. Donovan's ringer knows that information is more important than simply eliminating another loose end.

AMBUSH!

The gamemaster determines when the ambush begins, as well as the placement of Multitech's forces (see **Debugging**, p. 25). Those forces include a team coordinator, four troubleshooters, four snipers, and two combat mages. Once the free-for-all starts, the coordinator can use Smallville's closed-circuit camera network to track the runners and direct his own personnel.

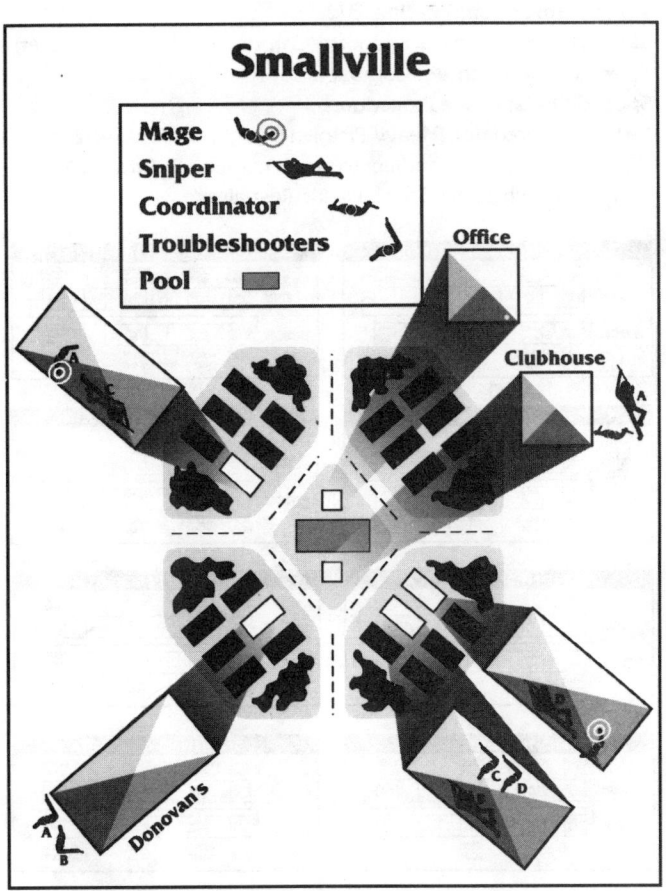

Coordinator

B	Q	S	C	I	W	E	R	Armor
4	5	5	4	5	6	4	5	5/3

Initiative: 5 + 2D6
Threat/Professional Rating: 4/4
Skills: Armed Combat (Edged Weapons) 3, Athletics 4, Biotech (First Aid) 3, Etiquette (Corporate) 4, Firearms 5, Interrogation (Verbal) 4, Leadership 4, Stealth (Urban) 4, Throwing Weapons (Non-Aerodynamic) 3, Unarmed Combat 4
Cyberware: Wired Reflexes (1)
Gear: Ares Predator [Heavy Pistol, 15 (clip), SA, 9M, w/2 extra clips, Laser Sight (–1 modifier to target numbers)], Armor Jacket (5/3)

The leader of Multitech's strike force, this individual will coordinate the ambush from the Smallville complex's clubhouse, staying in contact with his team via two-way headset comlinks. He begins the attack as soon as he gets the signal from "Dutch."

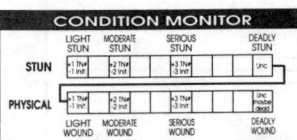

Troubleshooters (4)

B	Q	S	C	I	W	E	R	Armor
5	6	5	4	4	4	4	5 (7)	5/3

Initiative: 7 + 2D6
Threat/Professional Rating: 4/3
Skills: Armed Combat 4, Etiquette (Corporate) 3, Firearms 5, Unarmed Combat 4
Cyberware: Wired Reflexes (1)
Gear: Ares Predator [Heavy Pistol, 15 (clip), SA, 9M, Laser Sight (–1 modifier to target numbers)], Armor Jacket (5/3), Heckler & Koch HK227 [SMG, 28 (clip) SA/BF/FA, 7M, w/2 extra clips, Gas Vent II]

WELCOME TO MY PARLOR

Snipers (4)

B	Q	S	C	I	W	E	R	Armor
4	6	4	5	4	4	6	5	2/1

Initiative: 5 + 1D6
Threat/Professional Rating: 4/3
Skills: Armed Combat 3, Etiquette (Corporate) 3, Firearms 6
Gear: Armor Vest (2/1), Heckler & Koch HK227 [SMG, 28 (clip) SA/BF/FA, 7M, w/2 extra clips, Gas Vent II]

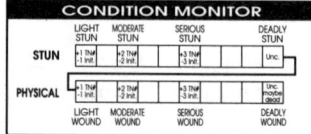

Combat Mages (2)

B	Q	S	C	I	W	E	R	M	Armor
3	4	2	5	6	6	6	5	6 (10)	5/3

Initiative: 5 + 1D6
Threat/Professional Rating: 5/3
Skills: Conjuring 5, Etiquette (Corporate) 4, Etiquette (Street) 3, Firearms 3, Magical Theory 5, Sorcery 6, Stealth 4
Gear: Ares Predator [Heavy Pistol, 15 (clip), SA, 9M, w/2 extra clips, Laser Sight (–1 modifier to target numbers)], Armor Jacket (5/3), Power Focus (4), Specific Spell Focus (Hellblast/3)
Spells: Hellblast 4, Mana Bolt 5, Manaball 4, Powerball 4, Powerbolt 5

Each of these mages has conjured two Force 4 fire elementals and a Force 3 earth elemental, putting them on "astral standby" until needed. Each of the fire elementals owes the mage who conjured it 3 services; the earth elementals owe 1 service apiece. In combat, the mages use the fire elementals to aid in the casting of their combat spells and keep the earth elementals in reserve to pursue the runners physically if they try to escape.

WHAT'S ALL THIS THEN...

With regard to Smallville, Multitech has a special arrangement with Morgenstern Security, a wholly-owned Multitech subsidiary. If the runners seem to be holding their own against the company troubleshooters in a stand-up fight, the coordinator can call for 8 private security guards as backup.

Security Guards (8)

B	Q	S	C	I	W	E	R	Armor
3	5	5	6	5	6	6	5	2/1

Initiative: 5 + 1D6
Threat/Professional Rating: 3/2
Skills: Armed Combat 3, Etiquette (Corporate) 3, Etiquette (Street) 3, Firearms 4, Unarmed Combat 3
Special Skills: Police Procedures 4
Gear: Ares Predator [Heavy Pistol, 15 (clip), SA, 9M, w/2 extra clips, Laser Sight (–1 modifier to target numbers)], Armor Vest (5/3), Club [Reach 1, 6M Stun], Plastic Restraints

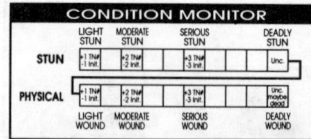

24 EYE WITNESS

WELCOME TO MY PARLOR

DEBUGGING

Multitech has cleared out everything of interest in Donovan's place. The player characters should know better than to come here at all, because the company would obviously muzzle their designer first. Even if Donovan were still present, he could tell the runners nothing new or startling. If the runners choose to show up at Smallville, they should swiftly realize that they are badly outgunned. Big-time hose-up, chummers.

If the troubleshooters overwhelm the player characters, they will bring any survivors to the Multitech Seattle branch office in Bellevue for interrogation (see **Lion's Den**, p. 38). If the gamemaster feels kindly, he can give the runners a chance to escape; otherwise, they will be questioned and then killed.

Clearly, the biggest possible problem in this encounter is the high risk of death. The gamemaster can handle this problem in a number of ways. If he wishes, he can ignore the **Hooks** section and tip the runners off to the ambush. For example, point out that Donovan lives in a corporate compound. Point out how quiet it is. Point out the hard-looking man pretending to tend a garden. Tip the runners off that something's up, and then see what happens.

Alternatively, the gamemaster can use distance and time to help the player characters. For example, he can position all of Multitech's forces so that, while some can get clear shots, their odds of hitting a target will be drastically reduced. Those who close the distance must take time to do so. This means that the runners should only face three to five members of the opposition at a time. If he uses this option, the gamemaster must balance distance and time in this encounter based on the strengths of the player characters involved. Pay close attention to the various Professional Ratings of the non-player characters, and remember that almost none of the opposition must be killed to take them out of the fight.

This encounter is designed not to decimate the runners, but to make the point that corporations can play smart, too. Multitech obviously knows they have a problem, and are taking active steps to control it. If the runners hope to succeed, they must work at it.

If the runners have not yet gone to Vanian's shop, go to **Vanian's Place**, p. 19. If they have found Vanian's address, go to **Rat's Nest**, p. 29.

SCENE OF THE CRIME

TELL IT TO THEM STRAIGHT

The corner of Leopold and Loeb…what a name for an intersection. Actually, it's a nicer neighborhood than you expected, even with a name like that. Anybody going half a kilometer in either direction had better have a purpose in mind, but the neighborhood right by Leopold and Loeb looks like a great place to raise kids. Nice houses, if small, with well-kept lawns. There's even a playlot, miraculously free of litter and broken bottles, complete with an intact swingset.

Half a block shy of the actual spot where Neil Scott bought it, you spot the rollers flashing in the distance. Lone Star is here in force. Time to rethink the plan, chummers…

HOOKS

Play up a sense of doubt and uneasiness about being here. Alpha Blue has reliable contacts in Lone Star; the runners have no reason to retrace the badge's steps on their own. If they decide to have a look for themselves, the gamemaster should make the player characters painfully aware of the presence of the authorities every step of the way. They should see flashing lights and blue uniforms around every corner. Hopefully, the runners will realize quickly that they are in the wrong place at the wrong time, and will leave before they get into trouble.

BEHIND THE SCENES

If the players insist on investigating the murder site, let them. They will find little of interest. Lone Star has cordoned off the site, of course: if the runners get careless, the cops will haul them in for questioning.

In addition to the investigating officer, Detective Rick Gordon, two cruisers are present, each driven by one trooper. If the runners do anything to annoy the cops or impede their investigation, the officers will give them the once-over, making Perception Tests to spot any concealed weapons. The troopers will confiscate any illegal firearms, and may even arrest any runner caught with one. If the runners figure on starting a firefight with Lone Star, forget it. The cops will call immediately for backup, bringing considerable reinforcements in minutes.

LONE STAR OFFICERS (2)

B	Q	S	C	I	W	E	R	Armor
3	5	4	3	3	5	6	4	5/3

Initiative: 4 + 1D6
Threat/Professional Rating: 3/3
Skills: Armed Combat 3, Car (Passenger) 3, Etiquette (Corporate) 3, Etiquette (Street) 4, Firearms 4, Throwing Weapons 3, Unarmed Combat 3
Special Skills: Police Procedures 3
Gear: Ares Predator [Heavy Pistol, 15 (clip), SA, 9M, w/2 extra clips], Armor Jacket (5/3), Club [Reach 1, 6M Stun], Plastic Restraints

On the scene for six hours straight without relief, these troopers are bored and tired, making them less efficient than under normal circumstances. Irritable from a combination of fatigue and tedium, they are unwilling to waste their time talking to scum, especially runners.

SCENE OF THE CRIME

DETECTIVE RICK GORDON

B	Q	S	C	I	W	E	R	Armor
3 (4)	4	3	5	6	6	1	5 (7)	3/2

Initiative: 7 + 2D6
Threat/Professional Rating: 5/4
Skills: Biotech (First Aid) 4, Car (Passenger) 4, Computer 3, Etiquette (Corporate) 4, Etiquette (Street) 5, Firearms (Pistol) 5, Interrogation 4, Leadership 6, Psychology (Deviant) 4, Unarmed Combat 4
Special Skills: Police Procedures 5
Cyberware: Dermal Plating (1), Cybereyes, Thermographic w/ Flare Compensation, Low-Light, and Camera; Radio Receiver, Smartlink, Telephone, Wired Reflexes (1)
Gear: Ares Predator [Heavy Pistol, 15 (clip), SA, 9M, w/2 extra clips, Laser Sight (–1 modifier to target numbers)], Armor Vest (3/2), Plastic Restraints

A survivor, Gordon has worked the streets for years. Whenever things got tough, he borrowed against his life insurance policy and ordered his surgeon to make him tougher. Despite being a middle-aged cop, he is walking bad news, respected and feared by both criminals and his fellow cops.

CONDITION MONITOR

	LIGHT STUN	MODERATE STUN	SERIOUS STUN		DEADLY STUN
STUN	+1 TN# -1 Init.	+2 TN# -2 Init.	+3 TN# -3 Init.		Unc.
PHYSICAL	+1 TN# -1 Init.	+2 TN# -2 Init.	+3 TN# -3 Init.		Unc. maybe dead
	LIGHT WOUND	MODERATE WOUND	SERIOUS WOUND		DEADLY WOUND

Talking to the cops poses plenty of risks for the runners. Detective Gordon might be willing to discuss the case with them, but only if they tell him who they are and why they care. Unless the runners can come up with a convincing lie backed up by a successful Negotiation (Fast Talk) (5) Test, Gordon will take them in for questioning. Undue curiosity about a murder arouses his suspicions.

WHAT LONE STAR KNOWS

Lone Star's ballistics experts think the sniper who killed Neil Scott fired a burst of explosive rounds from a FN HAR assault rifle, the explosives ripping through the top of the car to the target inside. The car's roof sustained heavy damage and two rounds found their mark, taking off most of the right side of Neil's head and ripping open his chest. He was killed instantly.

Extensive questioning of witnesses yielded vague descriptions of a sniper on a nearby rooftop. Lone Star's investigation of nearby roofs revealed little, but Gordon has a couple of long shots he hopes will pay off. A thermographic examination of the roof of an apartment block tagged a lingering shadow of the sniper's footprints, allowing the police to collect enough residue from the soles of his shoes for analysis. Investigative officers also found a few shells of seeds that the sniper must have eaten while he waited for his mark to arrive; they hope to extract enough blood from traces of the sniper's saliva to work up a genetic fingerprint. These clues will ultimately lead Lone Star to identify the sniper, but the process will take days. If the runners talk freely to the police, their information may help connect the sniper to Multitech, possibly leading to arrests and convictions. (Of course, how often do runners talk freely to Lone Star?)

If the runners discover the sniper's vantage point, they may decide to investigate the rooftop in hopes of finding some clue Lone Star missed. Unfortunately, they are drek out of luck. The Lone Star team did its work well, and not a shred of evidence remains for the runners to find.

JUST THE FACTS

If the runners can avoid running afoul of the police, they may question the neighborhood residents. Lone Star has been questioning witnesses for hours, but quite a few people unwilling to cooperate with the law might well talk to shadowrunners. If the runners ask around, they can find several witnesses willing to talk to them.

These witnesses report having seen someone on a rooftop overlooking the intersection where Neil died. Descriptions vary, however: no one got more than a glimpse of the sniper, and he/she was too far away to identify. Most of the witnesses describe the sniper as a big man in a long coat, carrying some kind of rifle. For each witness, the gamemaster should elaborate on this basic description as he sees fit.

During the investigation, several people mention a gentleman named Mortimer who lives just around the corner. They claim that he knows everything that goes on in the neighborhood, and suggest that the runners talk to him if they want to know the score. Gordon has never questioned him: unlike the runners, the cops know that Mortimer is full of hot air.

EYE WITNESS 27

SCENE OF THE CRIME

Mortimer

B	Q	S	C	I	W	E	R
5	3	4	4	3	2	5	3

Initiative: 3 + 1D6
Threat/Professional Rating: 1/1
Skills: Armed Combat 3, Etiquette (Street) 4, Firearms 3, Unarmed Combat 3
Gear: Club [Reach 1, 6M Stun]

A lonely man, Mortimer spends most of his time at his window watching countless dramas unfold in his little corner of the sprawl. Unfortunately, Mortimer is desperately friendly. Not only will he talk, it proves almost impossible to make him stop. Because he knows nothing save what he has overheard, talking to him is a waste of time. If the runners ask, he claims he got a good look at the sniper and invents a description of him as a big male ork with one red cybereye, wearing light body armor under a long, black coat.

CONDITION MONITOR

	LIGHT STUN	MODERATE STUN	SERIOUS STUN		DEADLY STUN
STUN	+1 TN# -1 Init.	+2 TN# -2 Init.	+3 TN# -3 Init.		Unc.
PHYSICAL	+1 TN# -1 Init.	+2 TN# -2 Init.	+3 TN# -3 Init.		Unc. maybe dead
	LIGHT WOUND	MODERATE WOUND	SERIOUS WOUND		DEADLY WOUND

THE WRONG MAN

The player characters may wonder why Lone Star is on the scene at all, given Neil Scott's status as a nobody. The sad truth is that a cousin of Mayor Schultz just happened to be a block away from the shooting when it happened, driving a Jackrabbit nearly identical to Neil's. Naturally, the Mayor's Office fears the cousin was the target, and so they are leaning on the Star. In turn, the Star is leaning on Gordon. Gordon knows it was a corp-related hit, and therefore feels no concern about the case. He is going through the motions to keep his bosses happy, but ultimately cares nothing about Neil.

As with **Welcome to my Parlor** (p. 22), where the runners go next depends on where they have been. If they have not visited Vanian's shop, go to **Vanian's Place**, p. 19. If they have Vanian's home address, go to **Rat's Nest**, p. 29.

DEBUGGING

Unless the runners do something really stupid, the worst that can happen in this encounter is that Gordon decides they are troublemakers and arrests them. Because Gordon has no charges that will stick, however, he can only detain them for a couple of hours and then release them.

The runners might also place too much importance on what Mortimer has to say. If this happens, they will start off on a wild goose chase for the mythical, red-eyed ork. The gamemaster should humor the players, inventing whatever details they need. They might even find an ork who matches Mortimer's description, resulting in a misguided confrontation with an innocent (and angry) metahuman.

EYE WITNESS

RAT'S NEST

TELL IT TO THEM STRAIGHT

Shady Hill Apartments is not the kind of place where you expect rats like Vanian to nest. It stands smack in the middle of a part of town they keep polished for the simsense travel tapes, and looks more like a pricey hotel than an apartment complex. Real marble in the lobby, wide-open spaces, oriental rugs that would keep you and ten chummers in high-priced drinks for a year...frag, Vanian must make a nice chunk of nuyen.

Maybe you're in the wrong racket...

HOOKS

Absolute, screaming panic drives this encounter, at least until the runners manage to get it through the fence's head that they mean him no harm. Vanian is normally calm and collected, but the sight of the Multitech team tearing through his shop blew his cool for keeps. He has holed up in his apartment ever since the assault, gun in hand, waiting for the hit men. He only recently had the presence of mind to call for help, and it has not yet arrived.

BEHIND THE SCENES

Strangely enough for such a ritz place, the building has very little security save for a guard station and a couple of cameras in the lobby. One of the runners must sign a register before the team goes up to Vanian's suite, but the signing is only a formality. The guards care very little about anything, as long as they get their pay.

SECURITY GUARDS (2)

B	Q	S	C	I	W	E	R
3	3	3	2	2	2	6	2

Initiative: 2 + 1D6
Threat/Professional Rating: 2/2
Skills: Etiquette (Corporate) 2, Firearms 3
Gear: Ares Predator [Heavy Pistol, 15 (clip), SA, 9M]

RAT'S NEST

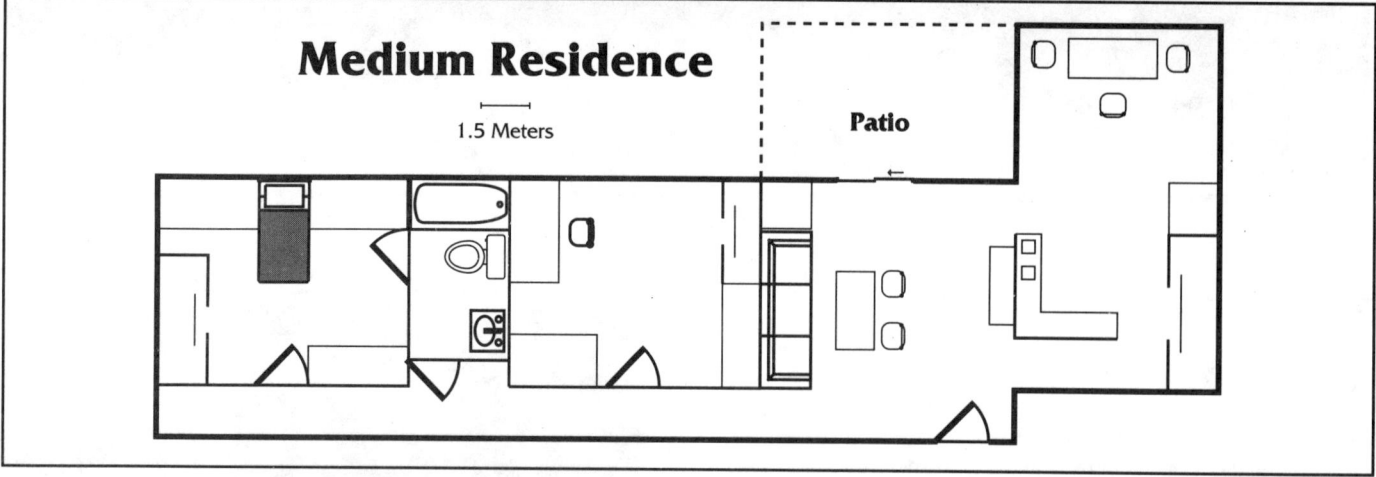

SUITE 2112

Having watched as the Multitech cleanup crew disabled his shop's security system and murdered his chummers, Vanian will have a tough time believing that the runners are friends. For all he knows, they may be working for the same people who knocked over his storefront. Vanian is so panicked that the runners will most likely have to resort to overpowering him in order to get him talking, assuming he does not manage to kill them first out of sheer terror. Once he sees that they do not intend to kill him even though he is at their mercy, he is more likely to listen to reason.

As one might expect, Vanian's suite is a hole. The gamemaster may choose what kind of hole. A slob like Vanian has no business mucking up a gorgeous building like the Shady Hill Apartments. Trash and junk lies strewn everywhere around his suite, along with the leavings of one or more small animals (hopefully pets). He has set aside a portion of his living room as a work area, though the runners can hardly tell it from the rest of the squalor.

QUESTION TIME

If questioned about the blueprint or the cybereye, Vanian is reluctant to reveal information about his clients but can be persuaded with threats or money if any of the runners makes a successful opposed Interrogation or Negotiation Test. (For information on opposed tests, see p. 68, **SRII**.) Vanian also tries to talk the runners into escorting him to his shop so he can collect a few important, personal effects before he skips town. Once persuaded to talk about the blueprint that Neil was working on, Vanian tells the runners the following:

"A punk named Breaker struts into my shop, puffed up like he just knocked over Aztechnology or something. Right off, I get nervous. His kind ain't my usual clientele. Gangbangers have trouble understanding the unwritten laws of supply and demand, and they have no tact. Dangerous bunch of jokers. He's wearing chains and warpaint that tag him as a soldier with the Iron Legion—also bad news.

"Putting Lou on alert with the silent alarm, I ask the kid what I can do for him. He gives me this grin, like I'm King Arthur and he has the grail in his duffel bag. He pulls a wad of napkins out of his jacket and starts unwrapping something. Noticing the blood and the chunks of meat dropping out of the napkins, I start to worry—know what I mean?

"He comes up with this eye—cybereye, thank the spirits, not meat. The eye is a nice piece of work. Nothing groundbreaking, but top-notch stuff just the same. Designer combined a natural look with a hidden camera, a tidy package of optics and microcircuitry. Popping it into a scanner, I notice the camera has an image stored in its memory.

"I ask Breaker what he wants for the tech. He pulls this little act for me, pretending to think about it. He wants to come off like a player, but the poor sap ain't got a clue. After some melodramatic eye rolling and chin scratching, he gives me a figure. Biting my cheek to keep from laughing at him, I haggle a little to make him feel better and finally accept his terms, telling him what a tough dealer he is.

"After the punk clears out of my shop, I tell Graham to watch the front. Then I slip back to the office and connect the orb to a dummy socket hooked up to a dataprinter to find out what's inside. The printer spits out this blueprint, that I can't make head or tail of.

"I have a couple of chummers on retainer who can tell me what I have and what it's worth. I sent the blueprint to one of them for analysis, but he ain't sent it back. Then the goon squad showed up and trashed my place. Poor old Lou and Graham, they never had a chance. I'm guessing the bastard ratted me out to somebody dangerous. I don't suppose you want to tell me where you come in?"

In addition to this story, Vanian can offer additional help. He maintains extensive records on all of his customers, including portraits pulled from his security cameras. If the runners ask for a picture of Breaker, Vanian will retrieve a chip from a desk drawer, insert it into a data reader, and run off a hardcopy on a high-resolution dataprinter.

By now, Vanian will also have realized that all this trouble revolves around the cybereye and the blueprint. Vanian has the eye in a box of spare parts on his workbench in the living room, and gladly gives it to the runners to be rid of the thing. An astute player character might note or ask about the presence of a serial number on the eye, which the runners can use to track the eye's owner. If none of the runners think to ask this question, the gamemaster should have one of the runners "coincidentally" notice it. For more information, see **Legwork**, p. 60.

RAT'S NEST

AMBUSH!

A team of Multitech thugs—four troubleshooters and a sniper—arrives shortly after the runners show up. The troubleshooters have orders to take Vanian alive for questioning, but have no reservations about killing the player characters if they get in the way. As soon as anyone tries to leave, Multitech's goons strike. If the runners sit tight long enough, the help Vanian called for will arrive: two street samurai and an elven mage. If the runners need help surviving the ambush, the gamemaster should bring these characters into play. For their statistics, use the Street Mage and Street Samurai Archetypes on pp. 61–62, **SRII**.

Troubleshooters (4)

B	Q	S	C	I	W	E	R	Armor
5	6	5	5	4	4	5.1	5	5/3

Initiative: 5 + 2D6
Threat/Professional Rating: 4/3
Skills: Armed Combat 4, Etiquette (Corporate) 3, Firearms 5, Unarmed Combat 4
Gear: Armor Jacket (5/3), Heckler & Koch HK227 [SMG, 28 (clip) SA/BF/FA, 7M, w/2 extra clips, Gas Vent II]

Sniper

B	Q	S	C	I	W	E	R	Armor
5	6	5	5	4	4	5.1	5	5/3

Initiative: 5 + 2D6
Threat/Professional Rating: 4/3
Skills: Armed Combat 4, Etiquette (Corporate) 3, Firearms 5, Unarmed Combat 4
Gear: Armor Jacket (5/3), Heckler & Koch HK227 [SMG, 28 (clip) SA/BF/FA, 7M, w/2 extra clips, Gas Vent II]

DEBUGGING

If Vanian dies before the runners convince him to tell them about Breaker and the Iron Legion, they will have reached an impasse. If this happens, the gamemaster can have Erin Scott call them with the information, or can invent friends of Vanian's who have heard the story. Once the runners learn of the Iron Legion's involvement, they will need to track down Breaker or another Legionnaire to get any further: go to **Party Town**, p. 32.

EYE WITNESS

PARTY TOWN

TELL IT TO THEM STRAIGHT

Welcome to Route 66, the flavor of the month. It's the latest blitz club, the 2050s version of the "rave parties" that have enjoyed sporadic popularity since they started back in the bleak innocence of the '90s. Toss together some portable mixing gear, a few hundred friends, and a public place, and you had an instant rave.

Blitz clubs work the same way, but with an important difference: they are conducted on private property, without the consent of the "host." Instead, the night's "club owner" hires enough muscle to secure the dance floor and defend it for a few hours. Trendy and dangerous, your average blitz is a who's who of street culture. Route 66 is one of the best of its kind.

Tonight the blitz is going down at Brighton Mall. By the time you get there, the party is in full swing. A troll stands at the door, and people are gyrating across the dance floor where the food court used to be. A capacity crowd hangs out in the stores, but no one touches the merchandise; pilfering is against the blitz club code. You know it won't be long before Lone Star shows up to pull the plug. You want to find who you're looking for, chummer, you'd better get moving.

HOOKS

Overload, chummer. People show up at a blitz club to get blitzed—on alcohol, chips, dancing, party spirit, you name it. Everything about this encounter breathes chaos and danger. If the player characters get overconfident, this encounter should remind them that the city has more and nastier surprises than they can ever learn to cope with. Keep the runners on their toes by describing all sorts of potential threats, both real and imagined: chipped-up razorpunks, nearby gunplay, and so on.

BEHIND THE SCENES

In this encounter, the runners are looking for members of the Iron Legion at one of the gang's known hangouts. If successful, they will discover the whereabouts of Breaker's girlfriend Emma, the only person who knows for sure where Breaker got Griffin Moore's cybereye (see **Black Widow**, p. 35). Unfortunately for the runners, Clean Steve and his muscleboys hit the Iron Legion hard scant hours ago, geeking a gang member for every ghoul that the Legion slaughtered on its ghoul hunt (see **Plot Synopsis**, p. 7).

GETTING IN

Like many popular nightclubs, Route 66 prides itself on being exclusive. Posers and curious wheezers slumming the downside don't rate high enough to cross the threshold. The doorman, a massive, ugly troll who calls himself Balder, decides who's hot and who's history.

Balder

B	Q	S	C	I	W	E	R
11 (14)	3	9	3	3	5	1	3 (7)

Initiative: 7 + 3D6
Threat/Professional Rating: 5/3
Skills: Armed Combat 3, Etiquette (Street) 4, Firearms 3, Interrogation (Verbal) 4, Unarmed Combat (Implants) 5
Cyberware: Dermal Plating (3), Retractable Hand Razors, Retractable Spurs, Wired Reflexes (2)

Immense even for a troll, Balder (aka Gordon Tufnell) works out with special equipment to sculpt his body into a musclebound nightmare. To enhance his threatening appearance, Balder wears only a loincloth and has riveted studs to his hide.

Though Balder wears no armor and carries no weapons, he openly displays the telltale scars and bulges of heavy-duty dermal plating as well as the housings of his retractable spurs and razors. Despite his lack of hardware, he looks almost as dangerous as he is.

CONDITION MONITOR

	LIGHT STUN	MODERATE STUN	SERIOUS STUN		DEADLY STUN
STUN	+1 TN# -1 Init.	+2 TN# -2 Init.	+3 TN# -3 Init.		Unc.
PHYSICAL	+1 TN# -1 Init.	+2 TN# -2 Init.	+3 TN# -3 Init.		Unc. maybe dead
	LIGHT WOUND	MODERATE WOUND	SERIOUS WOUND		DEADLY WOUND

Bribing Balder can work, but anyone brave enough to try it should not underestimate the value of the troll's endorsement. Anyone with the foresight to watch the door for a while will notice that Balder seems to prefer rough trade and attractive young people for the tough customers to ogle. If the runners dress tough or sleazy, they stand a better chance of getting past the troll bouncer.

Fortunately, Balder likes the look of the runners and lets them in without a murmur. If they ask the troll about the Iron Legion, he tells them he saw some likely-looking punks decked out in chains and warpaint, and advises the runners to check them out.

TIME TO MINGLE

Once the runners get past Balder, they enter a seething mass of humanity and metahumanity. Hundreds of people crowd the food court, thrashing to the insistent throb of slash-metal cranked

PARTY TOWN

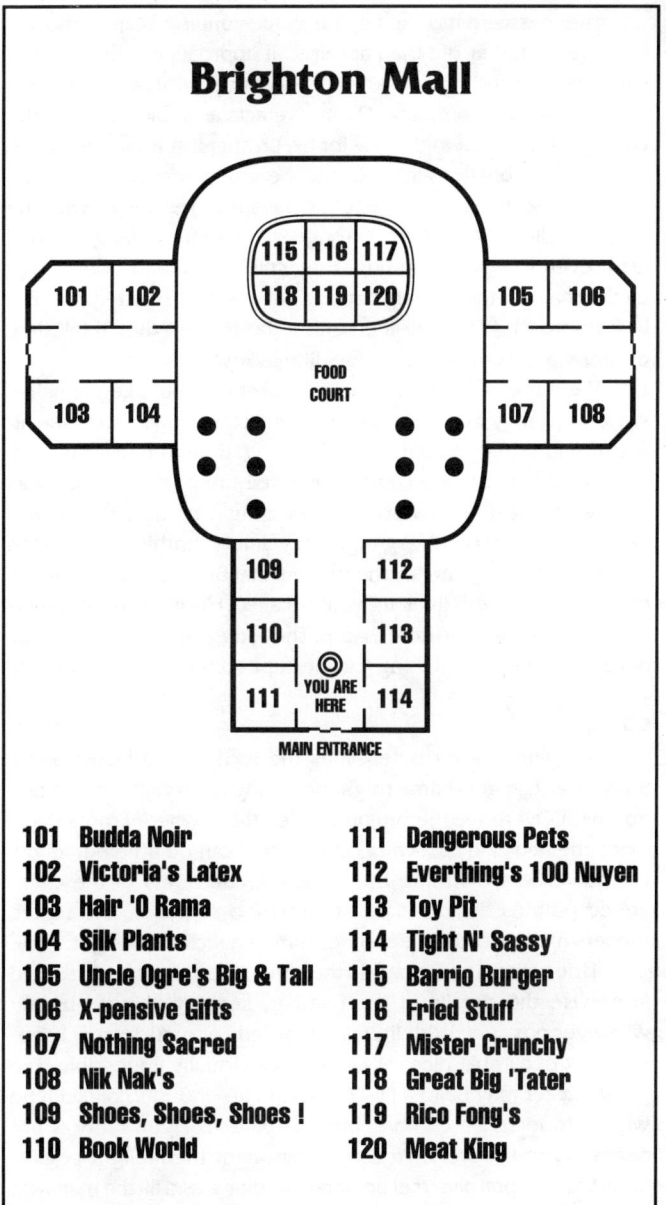

Brighton Mall

101 Budda Noir	111 Dangerous Pets
102 Victoria's Latex	112 Everthing's 100 Nuyen
103 Hair 'O Rama	113 Toy Pit
104 Silk Plants	114 Tight N' Sassy
105 Uncle Ogre's Big & Tall	115 Barrio Burger
106 X-pensive Gifts	116 Fried Stuff
107 Nothing Sacred	117 Mister Crunchy
108 Nik Nak's	118 Great Big 'Tater
109 Shoes, Shoes, Shoes !	119 Rico Fong's
110 Book World	120 Meat King

Iron Legion Punks (5)

B	Q	S	C	I	W	E	R	Armor
4	4	4	2	2	4	6	3	0/1

Initiative: 3 + 1D6
Threat/Professional Rating: 3/3
Skills: Armed Combat 3, Etiquette (Street) 3, Firearms 3
Gear: Browning Max-Power [Heavy Pistol, 10 (clip), SA, 9M], Club [Reach 1, 6M Stun], Synthleather Clothing (0/1)

Overdrive

B	Q	S	C	I	W	E	R	Armor
5	5	6	4	3	5	6	4	0/1

Initiative: 4 + 1D6
Threat/Professional Rating: 4/3
Skills: Armed Combat 3, Etiquette (Street) 4, Firearms 4, Interrogation 3, Leadership 3, Unarmed Combat 3
Gear: Ares Predator [Heavy Pistol, 15 (clip), SA, 9M], Club [Reach 1, 6M Stun], Heckler & Koch HK227 [SMG, 28 (clip) SA/BF/FA, 7M, w/3 extra clips], Synthleather Clothing (0/1)

In the good old days, Overdrive was a respected warrior who followed where others led. In the few short hours since the massacre, he has become the Iron Legion's new lieutenant. Though uncomfortable with the responsibility of leading his remaining brothers, he takes his new job very seriously.

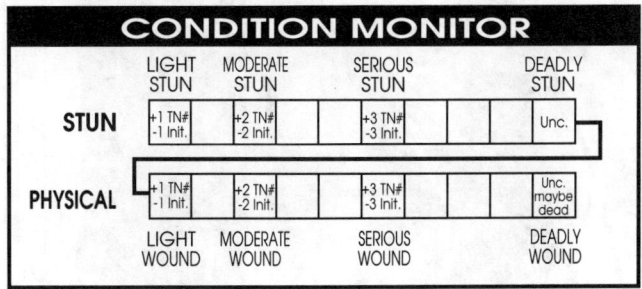

out by a wall of mismatched speakers. Moving through the crowd is a slow, awkward process; the runners cannot possibly get anywhere in a hurry.

On the plus side, the runners can meet plenty of interesting people. If the runners decide to mingle, the gamemaster should improvise a couple of encounters. Though such encounters should probably be inconsequential, the gamemaster should keep in mind that any number of important characters might be attending the party. Play with the runners: make them wonder who deserves their attention.

Clustered near Mister Crunchy in the food court are six muscular young men sporting the blue warpaint and chain harnesses worn by members of the Iron Legion. Normally, this breed of punk struts around like they own the place, but this crew is keeping an oddly low profile.

PARTY TOWN

The massacre has the Legion punks running scared, though they would rather die than admit it. If approached, the Legionnaires will let the runners know in no uncertain terms that they prefer their own company. Overdrive acts as spokesman for the gangers, laying down the law for his brothers. A lousy conversationalist who bristles with attitude, he grunts responses to even the simplest question. If the runners want to get tough with the gangers, discourage them. Strongarming a street gang is a bad idea; even if they are hurting, they still have their pride. Tough tactics may get the runners nothing but a bullet in the temple. The best approach is to give the Legion the respect they think they deserve, and wait until they feel like talking.

The runners' questions about Breaker make the Legionnaires suspicious: they may fear that the runners are connected to the hit squad that slaughtered most of the gang. If the runners can allay the gangers' fears, the Legionnaires tell them that Breaker was tortured to death a few hours ago during a particularly violent, professional hit on the gang. They know nothing about the cybereye, but they can tell the runners that Breaker had a squeeze named Emma who lives in a slum called Hope in the Puyallup Barrens (see **Black Widow**, p. 35). They suggest that Breaker may have told Emma something that he kept secret from his brothers.

CRACKDOWN

The gamemaster determines the moment to launch Lone Star's attack. A good time might be during the runners' conversation with Overdrive, before he can tell them where Emma lives. Once the raid is in full swing, the runners can do little but follow the panicked crowd into the streets. Quite a few of the club's armed patrons decide to resist arrest (no surprise), and so the runners must escape the dragnet during a vicious firefight.

If the runners participate in the battle, the gamemaster should improvise the details of the combat, keeping things abstract wherever possible. With literally hundreds of participants, keeping track of combat dice rolls will prove virtually impossible. The gamemaster may build a DMZ scenario around this conflict if he wishes to focus on combat, but this particular gun party is not necessary to the story. At some point after the firefight begins, Lone Star will pull back, set up defensive lines, and fill the mall with tear gas.

Once things go crazy, the player characters determine what happens next. The easiest way out is to blend into the crowd, dodge the badge, and vanish into the night. Defending the club will earn the runners some respect from the club regulars, but will probably also get them arrested.

DEBUGGING

Depending on how the runners handle the confrontation with the gangers, they may not get the information they need to find Emma. If this happens, have one of the punks get cornered during the Lone Star raid, giving the runners the opportunity to help him out. The grateful punk just happened to be on probation (surprise, surprise), and will tell his newfound chummers anything they need to know out of sheer gratitude for escaping the slammer. Once the runners learn Emma's address, go to **Black Widow**, p. 35.

EYE WITNESS

BLACK WIDOW

TELL IT TO THEM STRAIGHT

Buried deep in the Puyallup Barrens, Hope is a labyrinth of ruined buildings and battered modules salvaged from prefab apartments, held together with duct tape and spit. If the authorities gave a frag about this end of town, they'd have condemned the whole drekheap ages ago, but the city inspectors haven't paid Hope a visit since the last Ice Age. Neither have the cops. As you pick your way through the filthy streets of the slum, you feel hostile eyes boring into your back. It seems the denizens of this urban nightmare are trying to decide if they can take you down. Good thing you came ready to rock and roll. . .

HOOKS

Despair drives this encounter. From the rundown rathole where she lays her head at night to the remnants of her pathetic life, everything about Emma reeks of surrender. Make the player characters feel some of her sadness and sense of futility.

BEHIND THE SCENES

In this encounter the runners must find Breaker's girlfriend, the only remaining hanger-on of the Iron Legion who knows where the punk got the cybereye.

The Puyallup slum called Hope was built by people who wanted to disappear, so it often proves impossible to find anyone amid the urban decay unless he or she wants to be found. This rathole of a neighborhood has no addresses or mailboxes, and so the runners must ask the residents where Emma lives. The slum is infested with human and metahuman pests more dangerous than the rodents with which they share the scraps of food they salvage from the nearby soy plant. Anyone the runners approach may turn out to be the last squatter they ever meet. Just to make things even more interesting, the few locals willing to talk are reluctant to speak of Emma, frightened by rumors that a savage cat lives with her. The gamemaster should improvise a couple of derelicts, squatters, and the like for the runners to encounter and question.

After a few minutes of watching the runners amble aimlessly through the streets, the local riff-raff gets up enough courage to confront the team. A group of twice as many thugs as there are runners, led by two trolls, approaches the team. One of the trolls, acting as the leader, offers to show them Emma's house, but insists on an exorbitant finder's fee for his services.

LOCALS (UP TO 12)

B	Q	S	C	I	W	E	R
3	3	3	2	2	2	5	2

Initiative: 2 + 1D6
Threat/Professional Rating: 3/2
Skills: Etiquette (Street) 3, Firearms (Pistols) 3, Language (City Speak) 3, Stealth (Urban) 3
Gear: One packs a Heckler & Koch HK227 [SMG, 28 (clip) SA/BF/FA, 7M], two carry Ares Predators [Heavy Pistol, 15 (clip), SA, 9M] and the rest carry Clubs [Reach 1, 6M Stun]

Driven by hunger, these wretched squatters will do anything to survive. To them, strangers wandering around the slum represent an instant meal ticket. Unfortunately for them, the runners prove a tougher mouthful than the squatters bargained for.

EYE WITNESS 35

BLACK WIDOW

BENNIE AND JUNE

B	Q	S	C	I	W	E	R	Armor
8	4	7	2	2	3	6	3	3/1

Initiative: 3 + 1D6
Threat/Professional Rating: 5/2
Skills: Armed Combat (Clubs) 4, Etiquette (Street) 3, Firearms (Pistols) 3, Language (City Speak) 3, Unarmed Combat 3
Gear: Browning Max-Power [Heavy Pistol, 10 (clip), SA, 9M], Club [Reach 1, 6M Stun], Salvaged Armor (3/1)

Outcasts everywhere else, Bennie and June are VIPs in Hope. After they proved too stupid and volatile to work as bouncers, these twin trolls drifted downside and found their niche as leaders of the ragtag group of thugs that hunts this filthy little corner of the sprawl.

If the runners feel like wasting a few hundred nuyen they can buy off the locals, but the two trolls have hot tempers that make a peaceful resolution unlikely. Acceding to their demands looks to them like a sign of weakness and invites further abuse. Also, the trolls only take cash. Given these circumstances, the player characters may prefer to fight.

If the runners defeat the trolls and their riff-raff, they will find it much easier to locate Emma. They can either beat the information out of a defeated opponent or intimidate one of the terrified onlookers into spilling the info. Whoever gives the runners directions tells them to look out for the cat, but does not elaborate on that statement.

EMMA'S DOSS

After ducking under a corrugated aluminum awning and crawling through a section of rusted pipe, the runners find themselves in a tiny courtyard just steps away from a prefab apartment module with a red door. The door is locked, chained, and bolted from the inside. If the runners listen, they can hear breathing from the other side of the door. A runner with enhanced hearing can tell that the breathing is regular and shallow, and can also hear some kind of electronic equipment humming in the background. No matter how much noise the runners make, Emma refuses to answer the door; to get to her, the runners must break in. The bolts and chains give the door a Barrier Rating of 12.

Bedroom (A)

This room is small and dirty, but somewhat cleaner than the rest of the doss. When Breaker moved in, he spent some of the nuyen he had earned doing biz with the boys on making his crib more comfortable. Some of the furniture he bought new, and Emma actually made an effort to clean the place up.

Bathroom (B)

The bathroom is cramped and filthy. The shelf that serves as a medicine cabinet is piled high with over-the-counter remedies of every description.

Kitchen (C)

More a nook than an actual kitchen, this room includes such amenities as a hot plate, a breadbox, and a small ice chest on the counter next to a rusty filing cabinet that serves as a pantry. Some of the food has started to go bad, and the air smells peculiar. On a shelf are several bottles of cheap liquor, a Tiffani Self-Defender hold-out pistol, and a small box full of bullets.

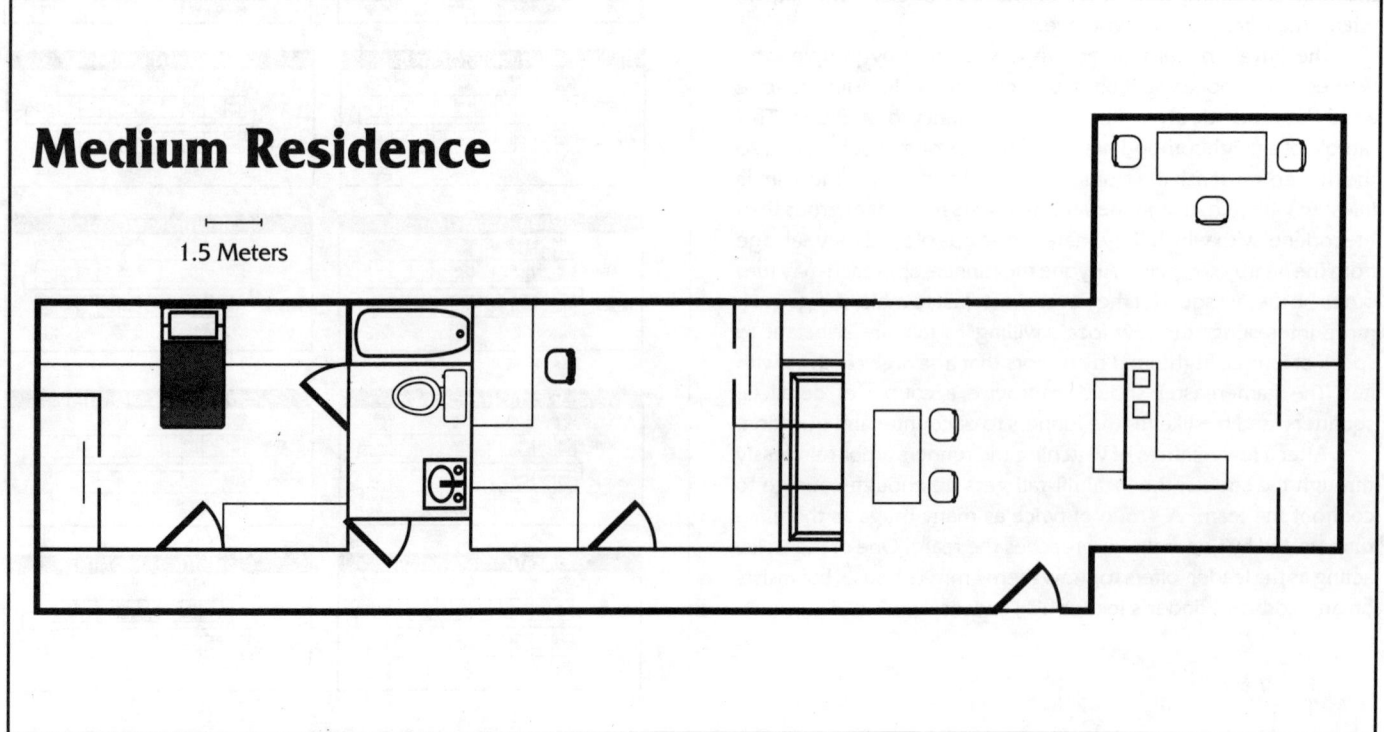

Medium Residence

1.5 Meters

BLACK WIDOW

Living Room (D)

Three battered, used couches form a semicircle around a pile of crates that serve as an entertainment center. On top of the crates are perched a vintage television and a boombox, along with stacks of stolen, vintage CDs and audio chips. Emma lies sprawled across a beanbag chair in the middle of the room, hooked up to a battered simsense deck. She is breathing slowly; her eyes have rolled back into her head, and she has developed a rhythmic twitch in her left arm.

SLEEPING BEAUTY

Like countless children of the sprawl, Emma was born to parents who abandoned her early on to the streets. Forced to survive on her own, Emma matured fast, running the sprawl for years until she found steady work recording cheap simporn. A year ago she met Breaker at a blitz club, and they fell in love.

When the Iron Legionnaires told Emma about Breaker's death, she searched her simsense tapes for a recording she had made of a vacation they took shortly after they met. Desperate to escape her present, unbearable reality, she spliced the tape into a continuous loop, disabled the safety features of her playback deck with an icepick, switched on, and tuned out.

By the time the runners arrive, Emma has spent two days watching her tape. For 48 hours she has had no sleep, no food, and no water. The runners can turn off the simsense deck simply by pulling the plug. Reviving Emma, however, proves harder. Emma's self-imposed ordeal plays hell with her frail constitution, leaving her dangerously weak. In fact, it comes close to killing her. For Emma's game statistics, use the Gang Member archetype on p. 57, **SRII**.

Savage Harvey

During her years on the streets Emma befriended a talis cat, a creature that can transform from a harmless-looking housecat to a ferocious cheetah. Even though Emma adopted Harvey as a kitten, she never managed to fully tame him. Unknown to her, Harvey crawls outside at night and feeds on luckless derelicts who wander into Hope. When the runners enter Emma's doss, Harvey is lurking in the living room.

Harvey

	B	Q	S	C	I	W	E	R	Attacks
Housecat	1	4 x 4	1	—	2/4	4	(6)	5	2L2, −1 Reach
Cheetah	7	9 x 4	7	—	2/4	4	(6)	5	8L2

Initiative: 5 + 1D6/5 + 4D6
Powers: Desire Reflection (Self, Cheetah Form Only), Enhanced Movement, Enhanced Physical Attributes, Enhanced Reactions, Enhanced Senses (Low-Light Vision), Illusion
Note: Treat the illusion power as a mask spell with a Rating of 12. It takes one action to activate the illusion power, at which point the talis cat may use the cheetah statistics. The second Initiative listed applies to the cheetah form.

Before the runners approach Emma, they must first deal with Harvey. The cat looks like a fat, white long-haired housecat, stupid and lazy. He hisses at the intruders: if anyone comes close, Harvey becomes a cheetah and bares his fangs in warning. If he thinks Emma is in danger, Harvey will attack. A well-armed team of shadowrunners can easily overcome the beast, but geeking Harvey loses them any shot at Emma's cooperation.

GETTING ANSWERS

If the runners display enough patience and sympathy, Emma eventually tells them whatever they want to know. She wants to know who they are, but will accept any reasonable explanation they offer, even a cover story as simple as "we're friends of Breaker's."

If the runners can keep her lucid for long enough, Emma will remember Breaker showing her the cybereye. When they ask where he got it, she tells them that Lone Star hauled in three Legion gangers a couple of weeks back, and the gang needed some quick nuyen for bail. They decided to go ghoul-hunting to pick up the city's bounty on flesh-eaters. According to Breaker, he found the cybereye on one of the half-eaten human corpses in the ghouls' sewer lair. If the runners revive Emma sufficiently to allow her to manage the trip, she can show them the manhole leading to the ghoul nest the Legion attacked. If the runners choose to hit the sewers, go to **Down In It**, p. 44. If the search for Emma comes up empty, the runners may choose to confront Multitech on its own ground out of sheer desperation: go to **Lion's Den**, p. 38.

DEBUGGING

The runners cannot go too far wrong in this encounter. Emma is so far gone that she will spill what she knows to anyone who gives her a sympathetic ear. If the runners alienate her by treating her roughly, fail to revive her, or succumb to Harvey, they can get the info on where Breaker found the cybereye via a call from Alpha Blue or a visit from Clean Steve.

CONDITION MONITOR

	LIGHT STUN	MODERATE STUN	SERIOUS STUN		DEADLY STUN
STUN	+1 TN# −1 Init.	+2 TN# −2 Init.	+3 TN# −3 Init.		Unc.
PHYSICAL	+1 TN# −1 Init.	+2 TN# −2 Init.	+3 TN# −3 Init.		Unc. maybe dead
	LIGHT WOUND	MODERATE WOUND	SERIOUS WOUND		DEADLY WOUND

EYE WITNESS

LION'S DEN

TELL IT TO THEM STRAIGHT

At first glance, Multitech's Bellevue HQ doesn't look like much. It's pretty enough—old-fashioned stonework from maybe a century and a half ago, smoky glass windows, flower gardens and a fountain in the courtyard. Nice. Ritz. Multitech must have plenty of nuyen, to pay the rent in this part of town. They probably also have enough nuyen to hide all kinds of nasty security measures behind that pretty facade. You've learned a little something about corps like Multitech, the outfits that produce cutting-edge tech on the quick-and-cheap to keep up with skyrocketing demand. Under that kind of pressure, only the ruthless survive—and Multitech seems to have no trouble surviving.

HOOKS

Think power and money, enough that Multitech has no need to advertise. This corp may not be Aztechnology, but they certainly have more resources than any piffling shadowrunner could hope to attain. If the runners take the risk of going straight to the source, let them know in no uncertain terms what a dangerous decision they made.

BEHIND THE SCENES

If the runners take the drastic step of dropping by Multitech's HQ, they have most likely decided to retrieve the information they need directly from the source. Unfortunately, the information no longer exists on the premises. As soon as Donovan reported the security breach regarding the flawed optical chip design, Multitech's troubleshooters went into action, eliminating every scrap of evidence. The runners do not necessarily know it, but they cannot acquire the rest of the blueprints from Multitech.

Of course, a Multitech run can serve other purposes. For example, smart runners might search for incriminating evidence of other nefarious doings and use it to blackmail Multitech for the information they need. Such a course of action poses incredible risks, but danger just doesn't faze some runners.

MULTITECH HQ LAYOUT

At first glance, the Multitech building looks innocuous. Set back from the street, it is a simple stone building that might have gone up around 1910 or so, with windows made of dark, opaque glass. Two rectangular flower gardens parallel the front of the building, and the large water fountain in the front courtyard plays constantly during the warm months. A simple sign with metal letters inset in the stone reads MULTITECH. Nothing about the facility's appearance particularly attracts attention.

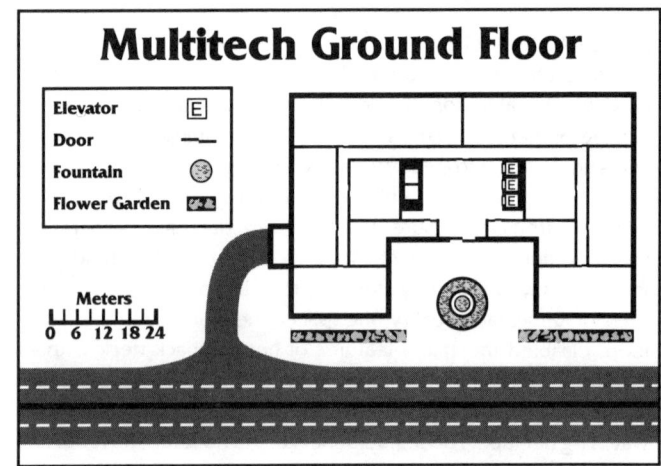

Reality, however, differs from appearances.

The "glass" windows are actually computer-regulated LCD crystals, programmed to restrict visibility into the building day and night, regardless of the lighting conditions. The doors are made of armored glass, and the windows have the same stopping power as the doors: both have a Barrier Rating of 8, and include armored shutters that raise the Barrier Rating to 14 when in use. The walls are also armored, and have a Barrier Rating of 24. On the ground floor, metal posts with a Barrier Rating of 18 rise from the ground to block vehicular access to the building through any navigable space between the building, the gardens, and the fountain.

The parking garage entrance on the west side of the building has a similar security system to protect that entrance in emergencies. A deployable cable system designed to foul rotors and entangle other kinds of aircraft protects the rooftop helipad.

LION'S DEN

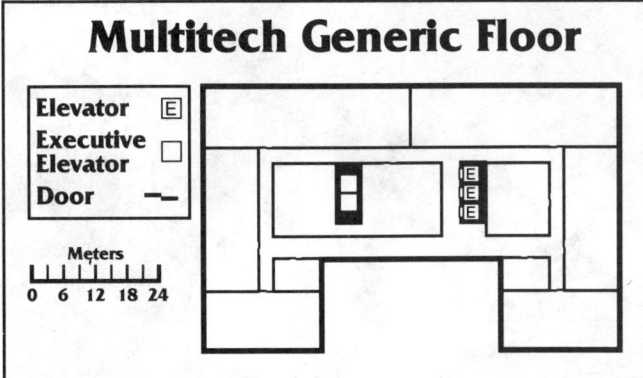

Floor Directory

The Multitech building has seven floors, five above ground and two below. Before running this encounter, the gamemaster should carefully review the map of the ground floor and exterior, the generic floor map, and the side-view graphic of the building that shows elevator access to the various floors.

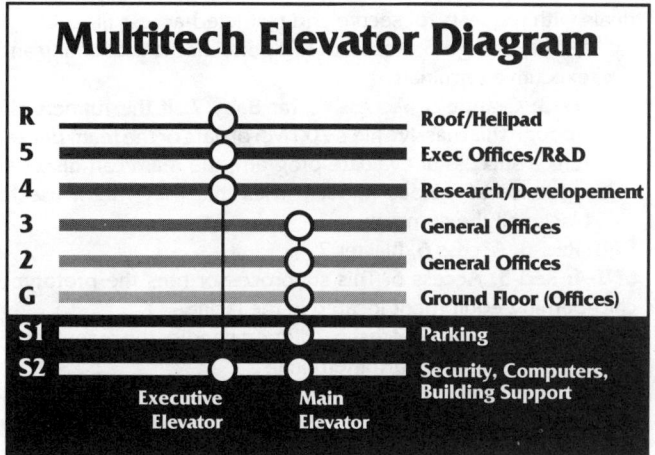

Security and Building Support (S2): This floor holds the building's security offices and its small armory, as well as heating and air-conditioning equipment, back-up generators, and other equipment necessary to maintain the building. In a well-guarded room across from the security offices is the heart of the building's computer system, including the CPU, all the SPUs, and all the datastores. Note that this floor can only be reached via the executive elevator. Employees on this level who wish to reach the 4th or 5th floors must use the executive elevator rather than the main elevators. To determine locations of rooms on this floor, use the **Generic Floor Map**, given above, as a template. Place the security and computer areas in the southeast corner of the building. The main elevators are those marked with an E; the executive elevators are represented by the two small, unmarked boxes across the floor from the main elevators.

Parking (S1): The parking garage covers this entire floor. Note that employees wishing to reach the 4th or 5th floors must go down to level S2 and then transfer to the executive elevator.

Ground Floor (G): An information booth and a reception desk manned by two security guards sits in the foyer; from this position, the guards can monitor all traffic through the doors. Accounting and administrative offices occupy the rest of the floor. Note that the main elevators will not descend to Level S2 without approval from the security offices on that level. For a description of the building's exterior and security, see **Multitech HQ Layout**, p. 38.

Second Floor (2): General offices (use **Generic Floor Map**, above).

Third Floor (3): General offices (use **Generic Floor Map**, above).

Research and Development (4): Multitech employees work on the company's most important projects in the work stations throughout the 4th floor. The southwest corner contains a shop filled with chip-burning and fabrication gear. To plot locations of rooms on this floor, use the **Generic Floor Map**, above; ignore the elevator bank marked with E to reflect the fact that only the executive elevators stop at this floor.

R&D/Executive Office (5): A continuation of the 4th floor, the 5th floor contains work stations for the senior designers as well as offices occupied by Multitech's head administrators and executives. To plot locations of rooms on this floor, use the **Generic Floor Map**, above; ignore the elevator bank marked "E" to reflect the fact that only the executive elevators stop at this floor.

Roof and Helipad (R): Accessible only via the executive elevator, the roof contains a series of condensers for the air-conditioning system, the concrete helipad, and a concrete housing for the elevator with a Barrier Rating of 24. Security personnel on level S2 control the executive elevator.

LION'S DEN

MULTITECH MATRIX

The luckless Griffin Moore managed to bypass most of Multitech's external security measures and access the Research and Development computer from the inside. Unless the runners gain physical access to a terminal in one of the labs or the office of a senior executive, any attempt they make to hack into the blueprint file will prove difficult, time-consuming, and dangerous.

Redesigned twice to accommodate corporate expansion and increased demand for more stringent security measures, the Multitech system's current architecture uses a series of layered subprocessors that force an intruder to penetrate several layers of IC in order to reach anything that might put the company at risk.

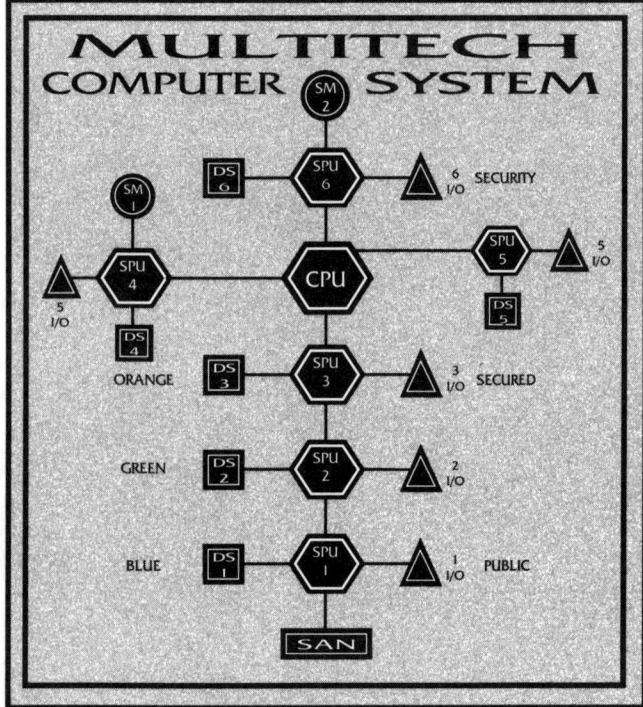

CPU = Central Processing Unit
DS = Datastore
I/OP = Input/Output Port
SAN = System Access Node
SM = Slave Module
SPU = Subprocessor Unit

SAN: Green-5, Access 5. This node is the only point of access to the Multitech system from the Matrix. The system's original architecture called for a second SAN to service SPU-2, but the second SAN made it harder to maintain security and so the execs scrapped it.
SPU-1: Blue-4. This subprocessor allows public access, and it therefore has little protection.
  I/O-1: Blue-4. This port runs the touch-screen terminals and data displays at the information booth in the building's foyer.
  DS-1: Blue-5, Access 6. This datastore holds nothing but public relations data used in the info booth's interactive displays.
SPU-2: Green-5, Access 5. This subprocessor handles most of the system's traffic.
  I/O-2: Green-5, Access 5. This port runs most of the terminals in the building.
  DS-2: Green-5, Access 5, Trace and Report 5.
SPU-3: Orange-5, Access 6, Trace and Burn 6. This subprocessor deals with requests for secure and restricted-access files.
  I/O-3: Orange-5, Access 6. This port runs the accounting and executive terminals.
  DS-3: Orange-5, Access 6, Tar Baby 7. If the runners sift through this massive file's 200 Mp of data or the team decker runs a successful evaluate program, the team can discover evidence of various minor crimes that they might use to blackmail the company.
CPU: Red-5, Access 6, Blaster 7.
SPU-4: Red-5, Access 6. This subprocessor runs the prototype chip-burning equipment located in the facility.
  I/O 4: Orange-5, Access 6. This port handles the manufacturing and system control terminals.
  DS-4: Orange-5, Access 6. This datastore contains the various programs and subroutines that run the chip-burning equipment, as well as back-ups of the layout files the burners use.
  SM-1: Green-5. This slave module is dedicated to the chip-burning and creation equipment.
SPU-5: Red-5, Access 6. Trace and Report 5. This subprocessor controls Multitech's research and development systems.
  I/O 5: Red-4, Access 5. This port serves the various terminals in the R&D sections of the building.
  DS-5: Red-4, Access 6, Trace and Dump 5. This datastore holds various chip files-in-progress. Of the 400 Mp of files, only 80 Mp have any real value.
SPU-6: Red-5, Access 6. This subprocessor is dedicated to the security system.
  I/O-6: Orange-5, Access 6. This port controls the terminals in the security office and in the senior executive offices.
  DS-6: Orange-6, Access 6, Trace and Dump 6. This datastore contains personnel files on every wageslave who ever worked for Multitech. The entry for Dutch Donovan states that his file has been transferred to the Shanghai office. The file contains the local access number for the Shanghai system, though without the appropriate passcodes. A dummy file for Griffin Moore also exists, protected by black IC and a Trace and Burn 4 program that activates if anyone tries to access the file.
  SM-2: Orange-5, Access 6, Trace and Dump 6. This module serves as the interface for the building's security hardware.

LION'S DEN

In addition to IC, Multitech employs enough deckers to keep two on-line at all times. For game purposes, treat them as Major League deckers with an Initiative of 6 + 2D6 and Threat/Professional Ratings of 5/3 (see p. 168, **SRII**). Note that the Professional Rating refers to deck damage. The first decker enters the system via SPU-6 when the runners trigger a passive alert. The second enters if the runners trigger an active alert. Statistics for the Multitech employees' decks appear below.

Fuchi Cyber-VI (2)
MPCP Hardening Active Memory Storage Load Speed I/O
8   4   100   500   50   30
Persona: Bod 5, Evasion 5, Masking 5, Sensors 5
Programs: Attack 6, Mirrors 2, Shield 2
Notes: Response Increase (1)

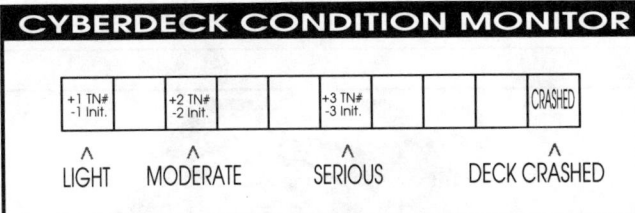

Hitting Shanghai

The architecture of Multitech's Shanghai system is identical to that of the Bellevue branch office, but the gamemaster should increase the ratings of all programs in the system by 1. The Shanghai system also has a third decker on-line in addition to the two Major League deckers mentioned previously. Treat this third decker as a Heavy Hitter (see p. 168, **SRII**), with an Initiative of 7 + 3D6 and a Threat/Professional Rating of 7/4. Note that the Professional Rating relates to deck damage. Statistics for the Heavy Hitter's deck appear below.

Fuchi Cyber-VI
MPCP Hardening Active Memory Storage Load Speed I/O
8   4   100   500   50   30
Persona: Bod 6, Evasion 6, Masking 6, Sensors 6
Programs: Attack 6, Mirrors 2, Shield 2
Notes: Response Increase (2)

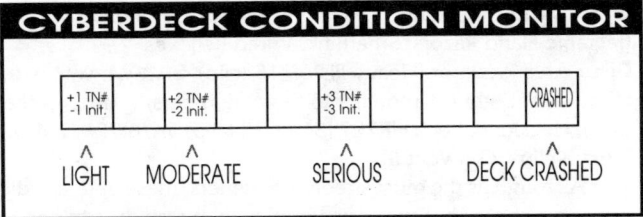

Shanghai's DS-5 contains the files Dutch Donovan is currently working on, which just happen to be corrected designs for the flawed optical chips. These designs constitute important evidence that can help Erin's case if she chooses to try extortion as a means of revenge against Multitech. They are not, however, required to complete the adventure.

ARMED AND DANGEROUS

Multitech's combination of top-secret contracts and shady business practices require the company to maintain an extensive on-site security force. Expensive and efficient, these boys are the best money can buy. The HQ is effectively an armed camp, and the runners should find it almost impossible to take head-on. If they try, they may face opposition of up to 28 people, including security guards, well-armed troubleshooters, and combat mages. The statistics for Multitech's various security personnel appear below. If more Condition Monitors than the 10 given for the security guards are needed, use one of the extra pages of Condition Monitors provided in the back of this book.

Security Guards (up to 20)
B	Q	S	C	I	W	E	R	Armor
3	3	3	2	3	3	6	3	5/3

Initiative: 3 + 1D6
Threat/Professional Rating: 2/2
Skills: Etiquette (Corporate) 3, Firearms 3
Gear: Ares Predator [Heavy Pistol, 15 (clip), SA, 9M, w/2 extra clips], Armor Jacket (5/3), Club [Reach 1, 6M Stun], Plastic Restraints

The bulk of the security force, these officers take care of such mundane concerns as checking passes. If they encounter anything more serious than an expired ID, they call it in to the security offices on Level S2, and the coordinating officers dispatch a troubleshooter team to deal with the problem.

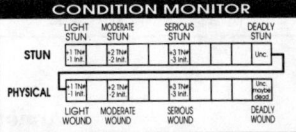

LION'S DEN

Troubleshooters (4)

B	Q	S	C	I	W	E	R	Armor
5	6	5	5	4	4	4	5	5/3

Initiative: 5 + 2D6
Threat/Professional Rating: 4/3
Skills: Armed Combat 4, Etiquette (Corporate) 3, Firearms 5, Unarmed Combat 4
Cyberware: Wired Reflexes (1)
Gear: Armor Jacket (5/3), Browning Max-Power [Heavy Pistol, 10 (clip), SA, 9M, w/2 extra clips, Explosive Rounds, Laser Sight (–1 modifier to target numbers)], Club [Reach 1, 6M Stun], Heckler & Koch HK227 [SMG, 28 (clip) SA/BF/FA, 7M, w/4 extra clips, Gas Vent II], Plastic Restraints

To protect its many secrets, Multitech's Bellevue branch office maintains a small, elite security force with a higher grade of training and equipment than the standard security staff. These troubleshooters, loaded for bear and deployed in four-man squads, deal with the serious drek.

Combat Mages (2)

B	Q	S	C	I	W	E	M	R
3	4	2	5	6	6	6	6 (10)	5

Initiative: 5 + 1D6
Threat/Professional Rating: 5/3
Skills: Conjuring 3, Etiquette (Corporate) 4, Firearms 3, Magical Theory 4, Sorcery 6
Gear: Ares Predator [Heavy Pistol, 15 (clip), SA, 9M, w/2 extra clips], Power Focus (4), Specific Spell Focus (Hellblast/3)
Spells: Hellblast 4, Mana Bolt 5, Manaball 4, Powerball 4, Powerbolt 5
Notes: Each mage has one Force 3 Watcher on call with three services.

Coordinating Officers (2)

B	Q	S	C	I	W	E	R	Armor
5	6	5	4	4	6	2.1	5 (9)	5/3

Initiative: 9 + 3D6
Threat/Professional Rating: 6/4
Skills: Armed Combat (Edged Weapons) 3, Athletics 4, Biotech (First Aid) 3, Etiquette (Corporate) 4, Firearms 5, Interrogation (Verbal) 4, Leadership 4, Stealth (Urban) 4, Throwing Weapons (Non-Aerodynamic) 3, Unarmed Combat 4
Cyberware: Cybereyes, Low Light w/Flare Compensation; Retractable Hand Razors, Smartlink, Wired Reflexes (2)
Gear: Ares Predator [Heavy Pistol, 15 (clip), SA, 9M, w/2 extra clips, Laser Sight (–1 modifier to target numbers)], Armor Jacket (5/3), Heckler & Koch HK227 [SMG, 28 (clip) SA/BF/FA, 7M, w/ 2 extra clips, Gas Vent II]

As tough as the most streetwise runners, these veterans did not come cheap, but they are worth every nuyen. In addition to coordinating operations against intruders, they train and maintain the on-site security force.

42 EYE WITNESS

LION'S DEN

ROOM AT THE TOP

Though it is unlikely, the runners may end up speaking to Maximilian Stern, a high-level Multitech executive whose statistics appear below. Such an event is most likely to occur if security forces have cornered the runners and want to question them, or if the runners ask to see someone with the intent of questioning or blackmailing them. Note that Stern is always accompanied by two bodyguards, whose statistics also appear below.

Maximilian Stern

B	Q	S	C	I	W	E	R
3	5	3	5	5	5	6	5

Initiative: 5 + 1D6
Threat/Professional Rating: 2/3
Skills: Computer 4, Etiquette (Corporate) 6, Etiquette (Media) 4, Firearms 3, Leadership (Commercial) 4, Negotiation 5, Unarmed Combat 3
Gear: Browning Max-Power [Heavy Pistol, 10 (clip), SA, 9M]

A third-generation corp executive, Max had his pick of multinationals upon his graduation from business school at the top of his class. He swiftly climbed the corporate ladder, becoming a senior exec in record time. The perfect corporate suit, he executes his duties with ruthless efficiency.

CONDITION MONITOR

	LIGHT STUN	MODERATE STUN	SERIOUS STUN		DEADLY STUN
STUN	+1 TN# -1 Init.	+2 TN# -2 Init.	+3 TN# -3 Init.		Unc.
PHYSICAL	+1 TN# -1 Init.	+2 TN# -2 Init.	+3 TN# -3 Init.		Unc. maybe dead
	LIGHT WOUND	MODERATE WOUND	SERIOUS WOUND		DEADLY WOUND

Bodyguards (2)

B	Q	S	C	I	W	E	R	Armor
6	5	6	3	3	5	4 (8)	5/3	

Initiative: 8 + 3D6
Threat/Professional Rating: 6/4
Skills: Armed Combat 5, Athletics 4, Etiquette (Corporate) 4, Firearms 5, Interrogation (Verbal) 4, Unarmed Combat 5
Cyberware: Dermal Plating (1), Smartlink, Wired Reflexes (2)
Gear: Ares Predator [Heavy Pistol, 15 (clip), SA, 9M, w/2 extra clips, Explosive Rounds, Smartlink], Armor Jacket (5/3)

Tough and brutal fighters, these bodyguards constitute the last line of defense for Multitech's top brass: in this case, Maximilian Stern. Their contracts provide a generous budget for cybernetic enhancement, of which they have taken full advantage. Following their standing orders, the bodyguards interact only with their superiors.

DEBUGGING

With all the firepower at Multitech's command, the runners can easily hose up big-time in this encounter. If things go really wrong, the gamemaster can introduce as back-up some of Erin's runner friends who have been shadowing the team on her orders. This miraculous save may seem too obvious, however, and the gamemaster may prefer to let the runners twist in the wind. After all, hitting Multitech was not the brightest move they could have pulled...and we all know what happens to people who pull dumb moves, eh, chummer? A gamemaster interested in teaching his players an object lesson might want to leave one or two runners alive: when they regain consciousness, they have a new scar, a cortex bomb, and a new boss...

DOWN IN IT

TELL IT TO THEM STRAIGHT

Once upon a time, you thought no place on this earth could be grimier or nastier than the downside of the sprawl. Wrong, chummer. Welcome to the Seattle sewers. Here you are, a team of first-string, primo, novahot shadowrunners, slogging through the river of filth that winds its way under the city streets. Some hotshots you are. You pick your way through the bilge and bits of garbage that you don't even want to identify, hoping that the scuttling sounds you hear are made by mundane rodents. A devil rat is all you need just now. Worse than the refuse is the stench, a cloying reek that makes breathing difficult. Lucky you don't have to run, chummer. . .at least, not yet.

HOOKS

Filth. The depths of a big-city sewer should be absolutely disgusting. Go all out describing the sight and smell of everything that gets flushed down a toilet or dumped into a river from a garbage truck. (Yes, everything.) By the time they encounter anything or anyone in all this drek, the runners should be sick to death of this slimy, nauseating underworld.

BEHIND THE SCENES

The runners are here to find some clue, however tenuous, as to where the cybereye came from, knowing that only by tracking it can they hope to find the rest of the optical-chip blueprints. One way or another, they need to find the ghoul lair from which Breaker took the eye: if any clues to the eye's source still exist, they will be in the lair. Searching the sewers proves a time-consuming process, as no map in existence will have the ghoul nest marked on it. This section intentionally does not include a map of the sewers: every tunnel looks much like any other, and the sewer should seem to the runners like chaos incarnate. To enhance the feeling of being trapped in a maze, the gamemaster should describe the tunnels, ducts, passageways, tubes, pipes, overflows, and galleries in bewildering profusion. The runners had better use something non-water soluble to mark their path. . .

Many of the city's ghouls live in the sewers, some under the protection of Adam Shepherd and some on their own. Knowing that he does not have the resources to control the entire sewer system, Shepherd deals with the underworld's other denizens and restricts the activities of his ghouls to a designated hunting ground. Largely because of this unspoken, territorial understanding between the ghouls and their fellow sewer-dwellers, the various loathsome beings that live in this foul environment tend to let each other alone.

Among the sewer rats of the two-legged variety is an underground gang of sorts who call themselves the Lost Boys. Though curious about the new arrivals, they initially lack the courage to approach the runners. Gradually, as they work up the nerve, the Lost Boys will gather until all eight are present. Unless the runners make the first move, the sewer punks will confront the runners the moment the boys outnumber them. The Lost Boys, however, are more interested in scaring the runners off than fighting them. In fact, a battle is the last thing the punks want.

Physical pursuit of the Lost Boys is a pointless exercise. The boys know the sewers far better than the runners do, and can quickly lose any pursuers. Astral pursuit, on the other hand, should prove successful, but will gain the runners little. Any astral pursuer will see that the Lost Boys are a rag-tag mix of gutter scum, lacking magic, cyberware, and any weapons more lethal than Ares Predators low on ammo. Should a runner choose to use magic in the sewers, note that the tunnels have a Background Count of 1. (For more information on background count, see p. 89, **Grimoire, Second Edition**.)

DOWN IN IT

LOST BOYS (8)

B	Q	S	C	I	W	E	R	Armor
4	4	4	2	2	4	6	3	0/1

Initiative: 3 + 1D6
Threat/Professional Rating: 2/2
Skills: Armed Combat 4, Stealth (Urban) 4
Gear: Club [Reach 1, 5M Stun], Heavy Jackets (0/1); two carry Ares Predators [Heavy Pistol, 15 (clip), SA, 9M]

These homeless gutterpunks have taken refuge from a society that rejected them in the maze of tunnels that wind under the sprawl like concrete bowels. They live off the waste of the surface world, raiding dumpsters near the entrances to their sewer home. Familiar with the many dangers that lurk in the sewer system, they have learned to rise above such threats.

The Lost Boys follow the runners because the runners are approaching the ghouls' hunting ground. Remembering that the last strangers to enter the sewers brought gunfire and slaughter, the Lost Boys fear that the runners may have come to finish the job or otherwise stir up trouble. Long isolated from civilized society, the sewer punks have no idea how to handle any social interaction; if they talk to the runners, they choose a spokesman to speak for the group. The spokesman uses as few words as he can get away with, stuttering if he becomes excited.

These punks know where the ghouls' lair is and keep well clear of it. Beyond that, they can tell the runners little. A few of them remember seeing people who match the runners' description of the Iron Legion gangers, but they do not recognize Breaker or any other individual specifically. They did not see Breaker take the cybereye, and do not know where it came from or if anything else was found with it. If the runners can convince the Lost Boys' spokesman of their good intentions, he offers to take them to a gentleman named Teacher, who may be able to answer their questions.

LEADING THE BLIND

The man the lost boys call "Teacher," an aged, blind mage, lives in a large chamber that once served as a cistern. The old man and the outcasts who befriended him have turned it into an apartment. Strange drawings of all sizes cover the walls, executed in different media from pencil sketches scrawled on scraps of paper to massive images painted on the concrete. All primitive, the drawings depict a reptilian face surrounded by a nimbus of stars.

As the runners approach the chamber, a hulking, robed figure accosts them and introduces himself as Abbott. He questions them before letting them proceed, asking them who they are, why they are in the sewers, and why they want to talk to "the master."

DOWN IN IT

Abbott

B	Q	S	C	I	W	E	R	Armor
8	3	7	3	3	4	6	3	4/2

Initiative: 3 + 1D6
Threat/Professional Rating: 6/3
Skills: Armed Combat (Clubs) 5, Athletics 5, Etiquette (Street) 3, Firearms (Pistols) 4, Stealth (Urban) 4, Unarmed Combat 5
Gear: Ares Predator [Heavy Pistol, 15 (clip), SA, 9M], Salvaged Armor (4/2)

An unusually large, rotund troll, Abbott has taken to wearing a brown monk's alb with a deep hood that conceals his goblinized features. Before the Awakening turned him into a hulking monstrosity, Abbott was the sole heir to a small corporate fortune. His patrician family disowned him after his transformation, and he had to fend for himself. When his money ran out, he lived on the street, where he met some of the Lost Boys. They took him to the sewers, where he met the old mage the boys call Teacher. Abbott became Teacher's bodyguard, and devoted his life to his master.

CONDITION MONITOR

	LIGHT STUN	MODERATE STUN	SERIOUS STUN	DEADLY STUN
STUN	+1 TN# / -1 Init.	+2 TN# / -2 Init.	+3 TN# / -3 Init.	Unc.
PHYSICAL	+1 TN# / -1 Init.	+2 TN# / -2 Init.	+3 TN# / -3 Init.	Unc. maybe dead
	LIGHT WOUND	MODERATE WOUND	SERIOUS WOUND	DEADLY WOUND

Alegheri/Teacher

B	Q	S	C	I	W	E	R
3	4	4	3	6	5	2	5

Initiative: 5 + 1D6
Threat/Professional Rating: 6/3
Skills: Biotech 4, Conjuring 4, Etiquette (Street) 6, Magical Theory 8, Sorcery 8

Born Gideon Alexander, the Lost Boys' Teacher now calls himself Alegheri. Years ago, as a young mage, his groundbreaking research into the nature of astral space provided much of the basis for modern magical theory. Intrigued by the apparent inability of magicians to leave the earth's biosphere without severe consequences, he decided to test and if possible transcend this limitation.

Alegheri believed that a magician's astral ability improved with practice, and that those who had died or suffered the loss of their magic on leaving the biosphere were novices who could not survive the rigors of extra-terrestrial astral projection. After years of preparation, he conducted what later become known as Experiment 231, the first attempt to astrally travel beyond the biosphere under controlled conditions. The experiment resulted in disaster, at least for Alegheri: when he regained consciousness, he gouged out his eyes with his bare hands. To this day, no one knows what he saw that prompted this act of self-mutilation.

Without vision, Alegheri cannot wield magic: ever since the experiment, he has had no desire to. Soon after the accident, his friends urged him to buy a pair of vat-grown eyes, but he refused. Whatever he saw on his ill-fated, astral journey, he had no intention of seeing it again. In the ensuing months and years, he gradually succumbed to a terrible fear that the open sky wanted to swallow him.

After decades of therapy to cope with his blindness and his fears, Alegheri fled the surface world, hiding out from the hungry sky in the labyrinth of the sewer system. He took his new name, and gradually earned the respect of the other denizens of the underworld. Many of the Lost Boys feel an almost religious awe of their Teacher, sensing but not understanding his latent power. Through an impressive information network of sighted followers and admirers, Alegheri knows everything that happens in the sewers, even though he sees nothing.

CONDITION MONITOR

	LIGHT STUN	MODERATE STUN	SERIOUS STUN	DEADLY STUN
STUN	+1 TN# / -1 Init.	+2 TN# / -2 Init.	+3 TN# / -3 Init.	Unc.
PHYSICAL	+1 TN# / -1 Init.	+2 TN# / -2 Init.	+3 TN# / -3 Init.	Unc. maybe dead
	LIGHT WOUND	MODERATE WOUND	SERIOUS WOUND	DEADLY WOUND

Friendly and exceptionally intelligent, Alegheri listens more than he talks, carefully measuring every word he says. If the shadowrunning team includes a hermetic mage, the old man directs his questions and answers to that player character.

If asked about the ghouls, Alegheri says, "Many live in the sewers who have reason to fear the light. The sprawl is no safe home for flesh-eaters, so they seek shelter in the dark. The surface-dwellers persecute them for having the bad luck to be cursed with a genetic time bomb. When I first came here, the tunnels were crawling with them: recently, however, they have withdrawn into a few, isolated enclaves. It worries me that they are becoming more savage: the few that my boys have encountered lately have acted positively feral. They seem to be losing the last remnants of their humanity."

If asked about the Iron Legion's hunt, Alegheri responds, "The punks must have been after the bounty on ghouls. My boys tell me they came rolling in bristling with weapons and went slogging through the murk until they happened on a ghoul lair. Then they opened fire, mowing the wretched creatures down in their homes. Three days after the raid, another party searched the same tunnel. Not gangers this time, though. A few of my boys thought they might be looking for something, but I can't imagine what."

Alegheri knows nothing about Griffin Moore's corpse, the cybereye, or the blueprints. He knows only what his informers tell him and what he might reasonably guess from their words, and they do not have that information.

If asked about the drawings or his reasons for hiding in the sewers, Alegheri evades the question and starts taking the drawings down. If the runners press the issue, he becomes agitated and may refuse to speak further with them, asking Abbott to see them out. If one or more of the runners decides to visit the sewers regularly and befriend the blind mage, Alegheri may one day confide in them, but he says nothing about the drawings or his past during the course of this adventure. For the purposes of this adventure, Alegheri can only point the runners toward the ghouls' hunting ground. He may tell one of the Lost Boys to lead them to the site.

HUNTING GROUND

If the runners venture into the ghouls' territory, almost immediately they encounter a scorched section of tunnel. Shepherd's team cleaned up this section in the wake of the Iron Legion massacre. Scarring on the walls indicates the use of a flamethrower, and divots from the explosive ammunition used in the battle litter the floor.

A little less than a kilometer further down the tunnel, the runners reach the ghoul lair. If they search it, they find that some of the nests are tied together with neckties: all are lined with the tattered remnants of expensive suits. These torn garments came from the corpses provided by Hammond Necroplex (see **Plot Synopsis**, p. 7). If the gamemaster wishes, he can drop the following clue at this point that will point the runners toward the necroplex as the next step in their investigation. He may have the runners find a mourning card in a still-intact pocket: this small card, traditionally given out at a wake, has printed on it the name of the departed, a brief prayer, and the name of the Hammond Necroplex. Note that this clue is one of two connecting the ghouls (and the cybereye) to the Hammond Necroplex. The runners can also find this connection by discovering the final resting place of Griffin Moore. No matter what, the runners must get at least one of these two clues.

The runners' search is interrupted (surprise, surprise) by a group of seven ghouls, three adult females and the rest children varying in age from five months to ten years. Unlike the saner, somewhat civilized ghouls that work for Adam Shepherd, these ghouls are feral, and frightened of the runners. Upon seeing them, the ghouls begin screaming and the adults move to defend the children. At this point, the runners must decide whether to kill the ghouls or try to calm them down in order to talk. If the runners choose to slaughter the ghouls, emphasize the fact that the player characters are killing women and children. Use the baby to drive the point home: ghoul or not, it is a young, innocent life cursed with its parents' genetic disease. Its nature is not its fault. Make it as difficult as possible for the runners to pull the trigger.

Once the screaming starts (especially if accompanied by gunfire), the rest of the ghoul clan comes running. Four arrive in every Combat Turn until fifteen adults are present. The statistics below apply to all the adult ghouls. If the children are shot or attacked with intent to kill, they die.

Ghouls (15)

B	Q	S	C	I	W	E	R
7	5 x 4	6	1	4	5	(5)	4

Initiative: 4 + 1D6
Powers: Enhanced Senses (Smell, Hearing)
Weaknesses: Allergy (Sunlight, Moderate), Reduced Senses (Blind)
Gear: Club [Reach 1, 7M Stun]

These wretched creatures, their minds twisted by goblinization, have lost most of their higher mental faculties and rely on instinct, hunting like animals. The moment they sense the presence of intruders, they attack without hesitation, hoping to swiftly overwhelm the enemy.

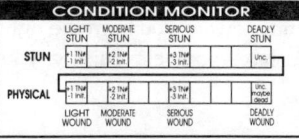

DEBUGGING

A slim chance exists that the runners will play smart and try to talk with the ghouls. After all, they may know something about the cybereye or the rest of the blueprints. If the runners make an effort to fend off the first round of ghoul attacks without resorting to lethal force and can convince the ghouls that they mean them no harm, the creatures may be willing to talk. Only a couple of them, however, can still speak English: and even these have suffered from their horrible transformation, making communication difficult. The best the runners can hope for is an invitation to Adam Shepherd's ghoul haven (see **Shepherd's Retreat**, p. 56). After all, any friend of the ghouls is a friend of Mr. Shepherd's.

EYE WITNESS 47

R.I.P.

TELL IT TO THEM STRAIGHT

Despite years of neglect, the Hammond Necroplex remains an impressive structure. The huge, gray, stone pyramid towers above the smaller buildings that surround it, throwing its cold shadow over them. Judging from its size, thousands of corpses may be permanently entombed in its concrete walls: it looms before you, a veritable city of the dead. One of the first of its kind, this grim monument turned a pretty profit until the past few years, paving the way for others like it that replaced the ground-eating boneyards of past centuries. For just a moment you think you can smell the odor of rotting flesh drifting toward you from the ugly, man-made mountain: then you shake yourself, cursing your overactive imagination.

HOOKS

This grim, desolate, post-modern cemetery is also the territory of a vengeful spirit. Use stark, unsettling imagery: describe the dark, empty halls lined with black marble and steel, lit only by the gas jets that serve as grave markers. Emphasize the contrast between the tiny lights and the looming, inky shadows. Make the runners hear countless footsteps echoing eerily off the walls. Describe some of the tombs they pass: improvise excepts from the eulogy tapes triggered by the runners' presence.

BEHIND THE SCENES

When businessman Jasper Hammond opened his necroplex, it was one of the first of its kind. Skyrocketing land values had placed burial beyond the reach of the average citizen's pocketbook, and turned alternative forms of interment into a necessary commodity. Pioneering efforts such as necroplexes changed the way society buries its dead.

The runners must cover a lot of ground, especially if they do not yet know exactly what to look for. In this encounter, they may run across important evidence in the Matrix system, a guilty exec hiding in the facility's corporate tower, and the free spirit that roams the Hammond Necroplex. Needless to say, exploring the massive crypt will prove a time-consuming prospect unless the runners have a clear idea of why they have come.

INSIDE THE NECROPOLIS

Regardless of how the runners decide to approach the complex, they should have little trouble getting in. After a sizable portion of the staff died in the spirit's attack, the rest have been understandably reluctant to show up for work. In the wake of that

massacre, Director Thaddeus Sinclair has called in what few security personnel he could induce to guard the complex, promising them double hazard pay.

Security Guards (4)

B	Q	S	C	I	W	E	R
3	3	3	2	3	3	6	3

Initiative: 3 + 1D6
Threat/Professional Rating: 2/2
Skills: Etiquette (Corporate) 3, Firearms 3
Gear: Browning Max-Power [Heavy Pistol, 10 (clip), SA, 9M], Plastic Restraints

Under-trained and lightly armed, the security guards patrol the facility in pairs. Already spooked by the deaths of staff members at the hands of the "ghost" that supposedly haunts the crypts, these guys would rather be anywhere else on earth. Only the hazard bonus makes them stay, and any hint of bad trouble may make them change their minds. Faced with any real opposition, they will fall back and call for outside help.

R.I.P.

Security Chief

B	Q	S	C	I	W	E	R	Armor
5	5	4	4	3	6	4	4	5/3

Initiative: 4 + 1D6
Threat/Professional Rating: 3/3
Skills: Armed Combat 3, Etiquette (Corporate) 3, Firearms 4, Leadership 3, Unarmed Combat 3
Gear: Ares Predator [Heavy Pistol, 15 (clip), SA, 9M, w/2 extra clips], Armor Jacket (5/3), Club [Reach 1, 6M Stun], Plastic Restraints

Only slightly more effective than the officers in his command, Security Chief Eric Lane served a three-year hitch with Lone Star before striking out on his own as a security consultant. Though well-trained, he refuses to endanger himself, preferring to coordinate the actions of his underlings from the relative safety of his security office.

[CONDITION MONITOR]

The greatest danger posed to the runners by the necroplex's ineffective, on-site security is that one of the guards may sound an alarm to bring armed reinforcements from Lone Star. The Hammond Necroplex has always had a mediocre security force, and maintains a costly contract with the local fuzz to compensate.

From the moment the alarm sounds, the runners must race the clock. The gamemaster determines when the reinforcements arrive: as a rule of thumb, the runners should get out before Lone Star shows up if they use their time efficiently. If they waste time inside the necroplex, let them have it. Have Lone Star catch them red-handed.

Lone Star Officers (6)

B	Q	S	C	I	W	E	R	Armor
3	5	4	3	3	5	6	4	5/3

Initiative: 4 + 1D6
Threat/Professional Rating: 3/3
Skills: Armed Combat 3, Car (Passenger) 3, Etiquette (Corporate) 3, Etiquette (Street) 4, Firearms 4, Throwing Weapons 3, Unarmed Combat 3
Special Skills: Police Procedures 3
Gear: Ares Predator [Heavy Pistol, 15 (clip), SA, 9M, w/2 extra clips, Laser Sight (–1 modifier to target numbers)], Armor Jacket (5/3), Club [Reach 1, 6M Stun], Plastic Restraints

Like the on-site security guards, these officers have heard the rumors of the necroplex "ghost." Unlucky enough to draw the short straw for this assignment, they feel extremely nervous about the possible paranormal threat. Their fear makes them trigger-happy: if they must enter the necroplex, they are more likely than usual to shoot first and ask questions later.

[CONDITION MONITOR x6]

Once the runners get past security (and possibly Lone Star), they may explore the pyramid at their leisure. They can learn nothing by questioning the guards. Neither the security staff nor anyone else employed by the Hammond Necroplex knows about the corpse-selling scheme except Director Thaddeus Sinclair, the man responsible for the scam. If the runners ask the guards about the Hammond disaster, they turn pale and refuse to answer the question, fearing that discussing the slaughter in the necroplex might rouse the spirit's anger.

If the runners choose to inspect recent tombs, they discover that one in three is empty. One of the empty tombs just happens to be the final resting place of Griffin Moore. Combined with Moore's records in the computer (see **Hammond Computer System**, following), this discovery provides sufficient evidence for legal action or blackmail against Hammond Necroplex, if the runners are so inclined.

The runners may also go looking for (or accidentally stumble over) Thaddeus Sinclair. The director and his bodyguard are hiding in his office on the top floor of the necroplex's adjoining corporate tower, from which Sinclair oversees the day-to-day operation of the Hammond Necroplex.

R.I.P.

Thaddeus Sinclair

B	Q	S	C	I	W	E	R
2	4	2	4	4	3	5	4

Initiative: 4 + 1D6
Threat/Professional Rating: 2/2
Skills: Computer 3, Etiquette (Corporate) 5, Leadership 3, Negotiation 4
Cyberware: Chipjack, Datasoft Link, Display Link, Fingertip Compartment, Telephone

A desperate man guilt-ridden over the deaths of his employees, Thaddeus Sinclair knows that sooner or later the spirit he offended will catch up with him. Though at first he tries to maintain the image of a tough corporate boss, when confronted with his crimes he breaks down and confesses, agreeing to cooperate with the runners in any way they wish.

Bodyguard

B	Q	S	C	I	W	E	R	Armor
4	5	4	3	3	5	6	4	5/3

Initiative: 4 + 1D6
Threat/Professional Rating: 3/3
Skills: Armed Combat 3, Etiquette (Corporate) 3, Firearms 4, Unarmed Combat 3
Gear: Ares Predator [Heavy Pistol, 15 (clip), SA, 9M, Laser Sight (–1 modifier to target numbers)], Armor Jacket (5/3)

After the spirit rampage, the terrorized Sinclair hired a bodyguard to see to his personal safety. Though a seasoned pro, if faced with an entire team of runners this chummer only puts up enough of a fight to satisfy his employer. He is not willing to die for his paycheck.

With regard to the corpse scheme, Sinclair tells the runners that he was facing bankruptcy when an anonymous patron contacted him by vidphone and offered to pay handsomely for fresh bodies to be deposited in a nearby sewer entrance. (He says nothing about the simporn recordings.) He has no idea of his silent partner's identity: he knows only that the payments came from a holding company called Berkley Management. After the spirit's rampage, the terrified Sinclair stopped selling corpses and hid in his office.

R.I.P.

HAMMOND COMPUTER SYSTEM

The runners may access the Hammond Necroplex's computer system from outside or inside the complex. No matter what point of access they choose, they will find the system tough to crack. When Hammond's director chose to break the law in order to break even, he became increasingly paranoid and spent a sizable chunk of Shepherd's loans to the company on upgrading system security to protect his secrets. The system has impressive security software; luckily for the runners, the director dispensed with watchdog deckers.

The Hammond Matrix System uses the UMS (Universal Matrix Specifications) image set. All constructs consist of interlocking geometric designs. If a decker triggers an active alert, the entire system shuts down within three Combat Turns.

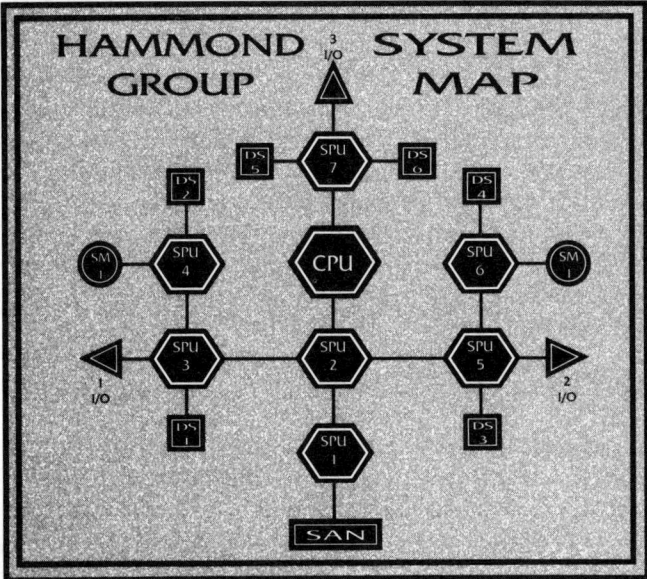

CPU = Central Processing Unit
DS = Datastore
I/OP = Input/Output Port
SAN = System Access Node
SM = Slave Module
SPU = Subprocessor Unit

SAN: Green-5.
SPU-1: Orange-6, Access 7, Trace and Report 7. This subprocessing unit functions as a security checkpoint, protecting the system from unwanted intrusion through the SAN.
SPU-2: Green-3. This subprocessing unit is a data junction that regulates communication between the two halves of the system and the CPU.
SPU-3: Orange-4, Access 5. This subprocessing unit serves the corporate office and handles day-to-day data traffic.
  I/OP-1: Orange-5, Access 6. This port connects the system to all terminals, monitors, and printers in the corporate offices.
  DS-1: Orange-5. This datastore serves as a data dump for unprotected files.
SPU-4: Orange-5, Access 5, Trace and Dump 6.
  DS-2: Orange-5, Scramble 6. This datastore contains restricted files.

SM-1: Orange-5. This module drives the air conditioners, elevators and security cameras.
SPU-5: Orange-4, Access 5. This subprocessing unit serves the necroplex building and handles day-to-day data traffic.
  I/OP-2: Orange-5, Access 6. This port connects the system to all terminals, monitors, and printers in the necroplex.
  DS-3: Orange-5. This datastore serves as a data dump for unprotected files.
SPU-6: Orange-5, Access 5, Trace and Dump 6.
  DS-4: Orange-5, Scramble 6. This datastore contains restricted files, including complete records of all individuals ever interred or cremated at the facility. If the runners have access to Multitech's personnel files, they can compare the two sets of files: this comparison reveals that Griffin Moore is the only Multitech employee entombed at Hammond Necroplex. The file also contains a copy of the interment contract and the location of Griffin's tomb. Alternatively, if the runners do not have precise information on Griffin Moore they can browse or sift through the files (depending on the programs they have) in search of a keyword, such as "Multitech," "designer," "optical chip," and so on. Eventually, they will discover that Griffin Moore, a designer working for Multitech, was interred at the necroplex around the time that Neil Scott bought it.
  SM-2: Orange-5. In addition to controlling mundane equipment such as elevators and security cameras, this module operates the "eternal flame" gas jets and recorded eulogies that adorn many of the tombs.
CPU: Red-6, Access 7, Blaster 8. In this system, nothing runs directly off the CPU. The seven subprocessing units handle all the traffic.
SPU-7: Red-6, Access 7, Tar Baby 8.
  DS-5: Orange-5, Barrier 7. Personnel records are stored in this datastore. The player characters may note that thirteen employees died on the same day, three weeks ago. This information confirms any rumors of the Hammond Necroplex disaster the runners may have heard.
  DS-6: Orange-5, Barrier 7. This datastore contains accounting records. Buried in the files are records of regular, 50,000-nuyen payments from Berkley Management to the personal account of Thaddeus Sinclair. Sinclair is listed in the personnel files as Hammond Group's Director of Operations.
  I/OP-3: Orange-5, Access 5, Trace and Burn 6. This port controls two terminals, one in the necroplex's security office and the other in the director's office. Though carefully protected, either terminal provides a handy "back door" that can make decking into secure areas of the system much easier.

UNQUIET SPIRIT

Unfortunately for those who perished in the Hammond disaster, Jasper Hammond constructed the necroplex without consulting magicians. Hammond cared nothing for magic, and his employees ultimately paid the price for his indifference. Unknown to the construction crews, they broke ground for the Hammond Necroplex over a locus of shamanic energy. Over the ensuing years, the burial ceremonies conducted at the facility inadvertently summoned a free spirit of immense power, calling itself Gallowgrey.

EYE WITNESS

R.I.P.

Gallowgrey is a unique entity, a tomb spirit. Though evidence exists of similar creatures inhabiting other burial grounds, Gallowgrey is the first known tomb spirit to have achieved freedom. Upon realizing that necroplex personnel were defiling the corpses in his care, a furious Gallowgrey went on a rampage to avenge the sacrilege. The systematic slaughter of the necroplex employees on duty that night was dubbed the "Hammond Massacre" by a sensationalist press: the necroplex shut down immediately afterward, ostensibly for repairs.

Within a day or so of the massacre, a surviving public relations wizboy came up with the explanation that a "chemical accident" had caused the deaths. Though this lame cover story could not possibly withstand close examination, the company spread around enough nuyen to ensure that neither the authorities nor the press asked too many awkward questions.

Gallowgrey

B	Q	S	C	I	W	E	R
8	9	5	7	7	7	7	22 (28)

Initiative: 22 (28) + 1D6
Powers: Essence Drain, Fear, Immunity to Normal Weapons, Manifestation, Paralyzing Touch, Petrifying Gaze, Search
Notes: The first Initiative applies to the spirit's manifest form; the second, to its astral form.

Gallowgrey usually appears as a white-haired, pale-faced, gaunt mortician dressed in a black suit. Initially, the runners may mistake him for an employee until they notice that his mouth does not move when he talks or they get close enough to see the strange, green glow in his eyes. A free spirit, Gallowgrey exists primarily in the astral plane and manifests only to attack.

The runners should find an encounter with the tomb spirit eerie and disquieting. If Gallowgrey believes that the runners pose a threat to his "children" (the corpses), the spirit will attack. If the runners can convince Gallowgrey that they have no intention of disturbing the dead, the spirit will return to the astral plane. Of course, if the runners have been prying open tombs, they may find it difficult to mollify Gallowgrey. More than likely, they will have to fight the spirit in its own domain. Given Gallowgrey's power, such a battle is a dangerous proposition.

DEBUGGING

Unless the runners have gone far afield before reaching this point in the adventure, they can and should find all of the information available in this encounter more easily somewhere else. The subplot with the free spirit is essentially background information, and has no direct effect on the runners' mission. Though Gallowgrey is an unusually dangerous NPC, he is bound to the necroplex pyramid. If the runners know the real score, they can easily avoid him.

Particularly clever and persuasive runners can make an ally of Gallowgrey, but the physical boundaries of his domain limit his effectiveness. If the runners have gathered enough clues by this point to figure out Shepherd's involvement in the adventure, they may persuade the spirit to avenge itself on the ghoul responsible for the desecration of its children. If they manage this feat, they enable Gallowgrey to leave the necroplex to pursue its quest for vengeance. Of course, the gamemaster decides how far the grim avenger manages to get in his pursuit. Gallowgrey may wipe out Shepherd's Retreat, if the gamemaster wants to play things that way. This possible outcome, however, will change the climax of the adventure. A gamemaster who chooses this option had best be prepared to improvise.

CONDITION MONITOR

	LIGHT STUN	MODERATE STUN	SERIOUS STUN		DEADLY STUN
STUN	+1 TN# / -1 Init.	+2 TN# / -2 Init.	+3 TN# / -3 Init.		Unc.
PHYSICAL	+1 TN# / -1 Init.	+2 TN# / -2 Init.	+3 TN# / -3 Init.		Unc. maybe dead
	LIGHT WOUND	MODERATE WOUND	SERIOUS WOUND		DEADLY WOUND

EYE WITNESS

EARLY HALLOWEEN

TELL IT TO THEM STRAIGHT

Club Nosferatu lies a mere ten minutes from the fabulous Regency Esquire Hotel. The hotel runs a complimentary shuttle bus to the club every hour on the hour: standing outside the club, you wonder why they bother. This is one weird place, chummer. Some slag converted a failed Mister Crunchy franchise into a faked-up church, and actually did a halfway wiz job. The facade is top-notch, right down to the moulded stonework and simulated, stained-glass windows. Still, you have to wonder about anyone who goes to a church to get blasted. Particularly a gloomy, raving-neo-gothic church like this one. Not much light shining through that fake stained glass. Now you think about it, those windows have an awful lot of red. Somebody obviously watched a few too many bad vampire flicks...

HOOKS

A parody of the post-modern club scene, Club Nosferatu reeks of stylish gloom. Turn down the lights, slip on a black turtleneck, and glower. The patrons revel in the agonizing grind of a meaningless existence: they have turned feeling sorry for themselves into an art form. The gamemaster can take the joke as far as he likes, or ignore it and play the encounter straight.

BEHIND THE SCENES

In this poser pit, carloads of rich kids dress in black and stalk about under the dim lighting looking gloomy and mysterious. (At least, they think they look gloomy and mysterious. Most of them actually look like they are having severe stomach trouble.) If the runners pay attention, they observe some of the patrons making surreptitious hand gestures to one another, using their own, primitive sign language to share their silent misery.

The drinks are watered down and overpriced; the music, though loud enough to burst eardrums, is almost impossible to dance to. (You want to dance in *here*, chummer? Why bother? Don't you know what a rotten world this is?) Tables near the back are shaped like casket lids. The entire staff wears head-to-toe black leather, adorned with the ankh that serves as the club's trademark.

YOUR FRIENDLY HOSTS

No one finds Club Nosferatu's clientele more ridiculous than does its owner, Baxter Attaway. Recognizing the moneymaking potential of the vampire subculture, Baxter figured to make a few nuyen by selling it to overeager, overly rich, overly bored consumers. Though ready to close up shop at a moment's notice when he feels he has crested the wave of the vampire fad, until then Baxter stands to amass a small fortune.

In public, Baxter becomes the gloomily handsome, I-dare-you-to-end-my-ennui Judas Caine. A bit of a frustrated actor, he plays the game better than most of the dark and droopy vampire wannabes that cross the club's threshold. He has even started a rumor that Caine is a real vampire, though nothing could be further from the truth. In fact, no vampire in its right mind would go anywhere near Club Nosferatu. They have far too much taste.

EARLY HALLOWEEN

Baxter Attaway (Judas Caine)

B	Q	S	C	I	W	E	R	Armor
3	3	3	6	5	5	5	4	0/3

Initiative: 4 + 1D6
Threat/Professional Rating: 4/2
Skills: Biotech (First Aid) 3, Computer 4, Etiquette (Street) 5, Firearms (Pistols) 4, Negotiation 5, Psychology 4, Unarmed Combat 3
Cyberware: Datajack, Retractable Spur, Telephone, Voice Modulator (Spooky Rasp)
Gear: Armor Clothing (0/3), Browning Max-Power [Heavy Pistol, 10 (clip), SA, 9M, w/2 extra clips, Laser Sight (–1 modifier to target numbers), Silencer]

CONDITION MONITOR

	LIGHT STUN	MODERATE STUN	SERIOUS STUN		DEADLY STUN	
STUN	+1 TN# -1 Init.	+2 TN# -2 Init.	+3 TN# -3 Init.		Unc.	
PHYSICAL	+1 TN# -1 Init.	+2 TN# -2 Init.	+3 TN# -3 Init.		Unc. maybe dead	
	LIGHT WOUND	MODERATE WOUND	SERIOUS WOUND		DEADLY WOUND	

Though most undead wannabes are a sedate crowd not given to the rowdy behavior that makes security so important in other drinking establishments, Baxter has nevertheless employed a few, top-notch people to ensure the safety of his patrons. Rico handles the guns and physical mayhem: Ariel deals with magical threats.

Rico

B	Q	S	C	I	W	E	R	Armor
6 (8)	6	6	4	4	5	.1	5 (9)	6/4

Initiative: 9 + 3D6
Threat/Professional Rating: 7/4
Skills: Biotech (First Aid) 3, Computer 4, Etiquette (Street) 5, Firearms (Pistols) 4, Negotiation 5, Psychology 4, Unarmed Combat 4
Cyberware: Cyberlimbs (both arms) [w/Increased Strength (2)], Hand Razors, Radio Receiver, Smartlink, Spurs, Wired Reflexes (2)
Gear: AK-97 [Assault Rifle, 38 (clip), SA/BF/FA, 8M, w/4 extra clips], Ares Predator [Heavy Pistol, 15 (clip), SA, 9M, w/2 extra clips, Laser Sight (–1 modifier to target numbers)], Combat Axe [Reach 2, 10S], Partial Heavy Armor (6/4)

Rico worked as a mercenary for years and had a local ripperdoc make him better than whole every time he took a wound. When he ceased to recognize himself, he decided to retire and took the job of bouncer/troubleshooter at Club Nosferatu. A consummate professional, Rico is courteous and efficient. He is also something of a ladies' man, and an unbeatable card player with the fastest shuffle in the sprawl.

CONDITION MONITOR

	LIGHT STUN	MODERATE STUN	SERIOUS STUN		DEADLY STUN	
STUN	+1 TN# -1 Init.	+2 TN# -2 Init.	+3 TN# -3 Init.		Unc.	
PHYSICAL	+1 TN# -1 Init.	+2 TN# -2 Init.	+3 TN# -3 Init.		Unc. maybe dead	
	LIGHT WOUND	MODERATE WOUND	SERIOUS WOUND		DEADLY WOUND	

EARLY HALLOWEEN

Ariel

B	Q	S	C	I	W	E	M	R
3	6	3	6	6	6	6	6 (9)	6

Initiative: 6 + 1D6
Threat/Professional Rating: 5/3
Skills: Biotech (First Aid) 3, Computer 4, Conjuring (Elemental) 6, Etiquette (Corporate) 4, Etiquette (Street) 5, Firearms (Pistols) 3, Magic Theory 5, Negotiation 5, Psychology 4, Sorcery (Spellcasting) 6, Unarmed Combat 3
Spells: Armor 4, Barrier 5, Chaos 5, Chaotic World 4, Combat Sense 4, Detect Enemies 5, Detect (Guns) 6, Increase Reflexes 4, Invisibility 5, Mana Barrier 5, Mana Dart 5, Mana Missile 5, Mind Probe 4, Ram 4, Sleep 6, Treat 5
Gear: Armor Jacket (5/3), Power Focus (3), Specific Spell Focus (Detect Enemies 3), Specific Spell Focus (Detect Guns 3)

No one knows Ariel's real name or where she came from, but no one doubts her magical talents. Though she has a gift for conjuring, she chose hermetic magic because its logical, ordered style suited her. In her capacity as Rico's assistant, she maintains the astral barrier that protects the club's office, and monitors astral space to prevent magical intrusion.

CONDITION MONITOR

	LIGHT STUN	MODERATE STUN	SERIOUS STUN		DEADLY STUN
STUN	+1 TN# -1 Init.	+2 TN# -2 Init.	+3 TN# -3 Init.		Unc.
PHYSICAL	+1 TN# -1 Init.	+2 TN# -2 Init.	+3 TN# -3 Init.		Unc. maybe dead
	LIGHT WOUND	MODERATE WOUND	SERIOUS WOUND		DEADLY WOUND

MEETING CLEAN STEVE

Clean Steve has chosen Club Nosferatu as a meeting place because Baxter is a good friend whom he trusts. Also, he once dated Ariel and trusts her implicitly. These associations make him feel sufficiently safe that he brings no additional muscle to the meet, but instead comes alone and unarmed. Note that Clean Steve has considerable martial arts training, and is therefore highly dangerous even without packing hardware.

Though Steve does not say who he is working for, he lets the runners know that his employer has interests similar to their own. In fact, Shepherd has told him to try to obtain the runners' copy of the missing blueprint. The ghoul has authorized payment for it of up to 50,000 nuyen: Clean Steve will open the haggling at 5,000 and work upward.

If the runners have any sense of honor, they will not sell out their employer. If they figure out that Clean Steve's employer has the rest of the blueprints, they may try to buy them. Keep in mind, however, that Clean Steve will not even confirm the blueprints' existence, let alone bargain for their purchase. Throughout the meet, Steve gives the runners as little information as possible. More than likely, this encounter will end in an impasse and an amicable parting of the ways.

The runners may well suspect that Clean Steve works for Multitech. If they ask him about it, he simply smirks and shrugs. If the runners choose to follow Clean Steve to find out who he really works for, the gamemaster must improvise any such encounter.

DEBUGGING

Clean Steve makes a dangerous enemy, so the runners should make every attempt to stay on his good side. As long as the runners remain civil, they cannot go too far wrong in this encounter. If, however, they pick a fight with Steve or anyone else in the club, Rico and Ariel can cause them real trouble.

SHEPHERD'S RETREAT

TELL IT TO THEM STRAIGHT

The offices of Agrippa and Associates stand on a tiny parcel of open land in the midst of a sprawling, industrial complex, stranded among towering manufacturing plants like scrubby bushes in a redwood forest. Installations the size of skyscrapers, some gleaming glass-and-steel towers, others concrete chimneys and festoons of metal scaffolding, loom over you as you thread your way toward your goal: Agrippa's walled compound, its tallest buildings no more than a few stories high. In the dim light from the overcast sky, the stacks belching black and white smoke look like a scene from Dante's Inferno. Compared to the smoking towers that surround it, the compound looks unimpressive, but you know better. You know what lies behind those walls, and you wish you didn't.

Welcome to the ghoul house, chummer.

HOOKS

Fear drives this encounter, on the part of both the runners and the ghouls. Obviously, the runners have reason to fear a compound full of flesh-eaters. Make sure the player characters know, however, that the ghouls fear them just as much. Despite the admirable defenses of the ghoul compound, everyone who lives there has dreaded the arrival of outsiders. To a ghoul, the average non-ghoul means only one thing: persecution and death. Monsters or not, the ghouls are far more vulnerable than the runners: regardless of the outcome of this encounter, the outside world will know the truth about Agrippa and can destroy the ghouls' haven. Play up the melodrama inherent in this situation.

BEHIND THE SCENES

No matter how the runners have chosen to pursue their mission up to this point, this encounter is one of the last events to occur in the adventure and may well be the story's climax. One way or another, the runners should trace the origins of the blueprint Alpha Blue gave them to Griffin Moore's corpse, and the remaining blueprints to the ghoul, Adam Shepherd. Alpha Blue wants revenge against Multitech, and needs the complete set of blueprints to achieve that goal. In order to get the prints, the runners must make a run against Shepherd's retreat.

Of course, breaking into the compound is easier said than done (no surprise). Thanks to his unpaid, ghoul work force, Shepherd has built Agrippa into an extremely profitable enterprise, giving him enough funds to pay for stringent security. Security measures include protections against astral invasion, a pair of lethally cyber-enhanced ghouls, a talented ghoul mage, and (of course) the great numbers of ghouls that live inside the compound.

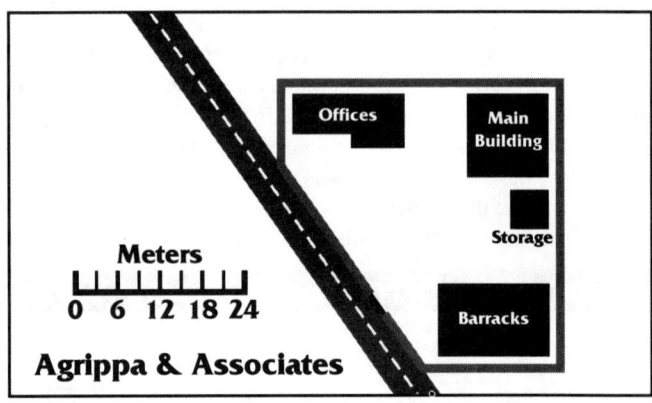

Agrippa & Associates

ASTRAL SAFEGUARDS

Creeping vines cover the walls of the compound and its main building, and moss thatch covers the building's roof. The living aura of these plants prevents astral travel into the building. In addition, several watcher spirits guard the entire compound.

If the team magician slips past the vines and the watchers, he or she must deal with the compound's inhabitants. Keep in mind that as a side effect of their transformation, ghouls have a dual nature. They cannot move astrally through physical barriers, but their innate magical capability enables them to spot an approaching mage easily.

SHEPHERD'S ENFORCERS

In addition to the overall ghoul population of Shepherd's sanctuary, the following three individual ghouls pose a particularly formidable threat to any group foolhardy enough to attempt a frontal assault on the compound.

Gog and Magog

B	Q	S	C	I	W	E	R	Armor
7	5x4	6	1	4	5	(.3)	4 (6)	8/6

Initiative: 6 + 2D6
Powers: Enhanced Senses (Hearing, Smell)
Weaknesses: Allergy (Sunlight, Moderate), Reduced Senses (Blind)
Threat/Professional Rating: 6/4
Skills: Armed Combat 4, Firearms 3, Unarmed Combat (Implants) 5
Cyberware: ActiveSofts (Firearms 3, Unarmed Combat 4), Dermal Plating (1), Skillwires (7), Spurs, Wired Reflexes (1)
Gear: AK-97 [Assault Rifle, 38 (clip), SA/BF/FA, 8M, w/2 extra clips], Heavy Armor (8/6)

SHEPHERD'S RETREAT

These two razorbrutes, Shepherd's personal bodyguards, owe their considerable stopping power to Shepherd's experiments with cybernetic enhancement of ghouls. In most ghouls, goblinization makes their nervous systems unreceptive, creating a poor interface with cybertech. The hosed-up interface produces feedback that can cause or exacerbate mental instability. Shepherd's scientists solved that problem by using sedatives and modified skillwires that allow the cybered ghouls to react instinctively, drawing on encoded expertise rather than on their own warped minds. In effect, cybered ghouls become unthinking, meat puppets who mindlessly obey their master. Gog and Magog seldom stray far from Shepherd's side unless he sends them to dispose of unwanted visitors (such as uninvited shadowrunners).

Nelson

B	Q	S	C	I	W	E	M	R	Armor
7	5 x 4	6	1	4	5	(5)	7	4	0/3

Initiative: 4 + 1D6
Powers: Enhanced Senses (Hearing, Smell)
Weaknesses: Allergy (Sunlight, Moderate), Reduced Senses (Blind)
Threat/Professional Rating: 4/3
Skills: Biotech (First Aid) 3, Conjuring (Elemental) 4, Etiquette (Street) 4, Firearms (Pistols) 3, Magic Theory 3, Sorcery (Spellcasting) 5
Spells: Barrier 4, Chaotic World 6, Hellblast 5, Power Bolt 6, Treat 5
Gear: Armor Clothing (0/3), Browning Max-Power [Heavy Pistol, 10 (clip), SA, 9M, w/2 extra clips, Laser Sight (–1 modifier to target numbers)] Power Focus (2), Specific Spell Focus (Power Bolt 3)

Nelson is one of the lucky few ghouls to survive goblinization with his sanity intact, and also one of the few of these dual-natured beings to be magically active. Having studied hermetic texts acquired for him by Mr. Shepherd, Nelson has become a competent mage despite his lack of formal training. One of Shepherd's most loyal followers, Nelson is slated to succeed him as director of Agrippa and master of the retreat in the event of Shepherd's untimely death. Nelson believes strongly in the cause of better treatment for ghouls, and will do anything to see justice done to his own kind.

OTHER COMPOUND RESIDENTS

The ghouls residing inside the Agrippa complex fall into two categories: enlightened ghouls who have retained their sanity, and feral ghouls driven insane by their ghastly transformation. All of the residents will fight fiercely to protect the compound if they feel that the runners threaten their safety. For the feral ghouls, use the Condition Monitors in the back of this book.

Enlightened Ghouls (12)

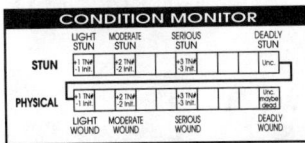

B	Q	S	C	I	W	E	R
7	5 x 4	6	1	4	5	(5)	4

Initiative: 4 + 1D6
Powers: Enhanced Senses (Hearing, Smell)
Weaknesses: Allergy (Sunlight, Moderate), Reduced Senses (Blind)
Threat/Professional Rating: 3/2
Skills: Armed Combat 3, Firearms 3, Unarmed Combat 3
Gear: Ares Predator [Heavy Pistol, 15 (clip), SA, 9M, w/1 extra clip], Armor Vest (2/1), Club [Reach 1, 7M Stun]

These few ghouls, fortunate enough to escape the dehumanizing insanity that turns most ghouls into bloodthirsty beasts, have become part of Shepherd's elite. Blessed with superhuman abilities and armed with lethal, black-market weapons, they make formidable opponents.

SHEPHERD'S RETREAT

Feral Ghouls (30)

B	Q	S	C	I	W	E	R
7	5 x 4	6	1	4	5	(5)	4

Initiative: 4 + 1D6
Powers: Enhanced Senses (Hearing, Smell)
Weaknesses: Allergy (Sunlight, Moderate), Reduced Senses (Blind)

These poor creatures suffered permanent mental trauma from their agonizing transformation. Little better than beasts, they couple animal instinct with human cunning to make them excellent and dangerous hunters. Though normally confined to the underworld that Shepherd built for them beneath the compound, these feral ghouls will be released if the compound comes under heavy fire. They carry no weapons, but their sheer numbers should make any attacker think twice.

CALLING OFF THE DOGS

Despite the sheer number of ghouls in the complex, the runners just might get the upper hand if they wade in with guns blazing. If they kill a dozen or more ghouls and seem likely to win the battle, Shepherd will call for a cease-fire. Rather than see his ghouls killed, Shepherd will beg the runners to meet with him so that they can figure out a peaceful resolution to the conflict.

MEETING SHEPHERD

Regardless of when and under what circumstances the runners meet Shepherd, they find him disarmingly polite. Shepherd wants more than anything to prove that his people are capable of civilized behavior, and considers himself an exemplar of the best side of ghoul nature.

If the runners give him a chance to talk, Shepherd will explain to them what he hopes to achieve for his people. A persuasive speaker, Shepherd may be able to win the runners' sympathy, but will have difficulty talking them into surrendering the blueprint he needs to achieve his goals. After all, the runners cannot get paid unless Alpha Blue gets all the blueprints, and she intends to take Multitech down once she has her evidence. Shepherd, however, needs Multitech to survive and prosper in order to profit from it.

Shepherd refuses to surrender his blueprints unless his people are threatened. Depending on how the runners feel about slaughtering innocents, they can either try strongarm tactics or attempt to steal the prints. The blueprints are stored in a safe-deposit box: in order to steal them, the runners must find the key hidden in the kitchen of the compound's main building. Given that the runners do not know precisely where to find the safe-deposit box, this outcome is unlikely.

DEBUGGING

This encounter has no quick fix or fallback. Either the runners get the blueprints from Shepherd, or they fail. The runners can either kill for the prints (likely), rip them off (unlikely), or try a third angle: blackmail. If the runners figure out enough about Shepherd and the compound he calls the Retreat, they can probably get the blueprints by threatening to expose the ghouls. Time to play hardball, chummers.

If the group decides to give Shepherd what he wants, Alpha Blue will eventually find out. Not one to take betrayal lying down, she will make it her business to see that the runners never get another decent job. If the runners choose this course, they should seriously contemplate relocating.

Keep in mind that Seattle currently pays a bounty of 100 nuyen per male ghoul and 150 nuyen per female. Roughly 30 percent of the ghouls in the compound are female. Give those figures to the runners, and let them think about it.

PICKING UP THE PIECES

This section provides information the gamemaster can use to wrap up all the adventure's loose ends.

AFTER THE ADVENTURE

Alpha Blue wants one thing: revenge against Multitech. The only way she can get it is by obtaining the complete set of blueprints for the flawed optical chip. The only way to get the blueprints is through Shepherd, who will not give them up unless forced to.

Once the runners obtain the blueprints, they need only deliver them to Alpha Blue to wrap up the adventure. That's it—no big gunfight, no nothing. Blue takes the plans and pays the runners. Her vengeance is private, and the runners do not participate in it (unless the gamemaster wants to extend the adventure.)

If the runners fail to obtain the blueprints, the consequences of that failure depend on Alpha Blue. She may decide that the runners gave it their best shot, and failed because of circumstances beyond their control; alternatively, she may regard them as a lousy bunch of hose-ups who ought never to get a job again. The gamemaster should determine Alpha Blue's reaction to failure based on how well the players played the game. If the runners hose up because of stupidity, let Alpha Blue do her worst.

KARMA

Award individual Karma Points per the guidelines on page 199, **SRII**. Award team Karma as follows:

Alpha Blue obtains the complete set of blueprints	6
Alpha Blue and Shepherd reach a deal	8
The team clears Gibson Hall of innocents or defuses the bomb	1

EYE WITNESS

LEGWORK

To follow up on or discover clues in this adventure, the player characters need to investigate people, places, and situations. One of the best ways for runners to get the information they need is through their contacts. This section provides success tables containing information available to the runners from their sources.

A success test using Street or Corporate Etiquette, Target Number 4, typically serves to find out what a contact does or does not know. The amount of information available from the contact depends on the number of successes the player achieves. Characters who achieve more than one success gain all the information available to all previous levels of success.

The gamemaster should try to make the player character's interaction with his contact consist of more than a few abstract die rolls. Play out the meeting in full: contacts are characters with their own lives, points of view, and needs, not simply spigots of information to be turned on and off automatically.

The player character rolls a number of dice equal to his Etiquette Skill to determine what information the contact knows and is willing to impart. Once the number of successes is determined, the gamemaster can roleplay the encounter with the appropriate information level in mind. Meetings should be tailored to the "personality" of specific contacts. Some will prefer a straightforward meet in a specific place, while others will only feel comfortable with elaborate forms of information exchange.

Contacts are generally considered trustworthy, as long as the runners play it safe and do not compromise their sources by revealing their sources' identities. Are the contact's ties stronger to his group or to the runner? A good runner never tests those ties by placing his contact in a position where he must choose.

Dealing with contacts is a two-way street. Most contacts want something in return for their help. Gamemasters who need a baseline value to determine fees for information can use the following formula. Multiply the contact's Skill Rating in his or her most appropriate Etiquette by the number of successes the player rolled in his Etiquette Test. Multiply that total by the sum of the contact's Charisma and Intelligence. Then multiply that final value by 10. The result is in nuyen. Gamemasters will, of course, adjust the base result to reflect the actual contact involved. Normal Negotiation procedures apply to determine the final payment for the information.

Runners may also ask their contacts to "check around" or "keep their ear to the ground," or some other idiom describing generally listening for news. In such a case, the gamemaster makes an appropriate Etiquette Test for the contact at +2 against the target number given in the information table. If the Etiquette Test results in any successes, the contact reports the appropriate information to the runner in 2D6 hours, or at a time determined by

the gamemaster. This is an excellent way for gamemasters to make sure that the runners learn a certain piece of information. The cost of this service is determined as if the contact had access to the information initially.

The gamemaster can add complexity to legwork by acknowledging that contacts are not always available at the convenience of the runners. Arrangements must be made before the actual meeting can take place. When a player character wants to meet with a contact, the gamemaster rolls 2D6, then multiplies the result by 30. The resulting base time is the number of minutes it will take to arrange the meeting with the contact. Players may elect to trade off successes from their Etiquette Test to reduce the time it takes to reach the contact and so receive faster, but potentially less helpful, information. In this case, the gamemaster can have the player make the character's Etiquette Test at the time he announces his intention to meet with the contact. The player should also decide at that time how many successes he will trade off to reduce the waiting period. The base time value should be kept secret.

LEGWORK

ELECTRONIC LEGWORK

Deckers may also take an active role in acquiring general information. Many electronic information services exist in the era of **Shadowrun**—public, private, and secret—and these contain gigapulses of data comprised of on-line conversations, rumors, stolen and dumped files, and the like. Deckers can create simple programs to search vast databases for key words and related terms, then download the information to their cyberdeck or Matrix-connected personal computer. Gamemasters should assume that all deckers have such a program.

Virtually any information available in this section can be found in the Matrix, provided one knows where to look and has the time. The base time for such a search is 2D6 hours. The decker makes a success test against his or her Etiquette (Matrix) Skill, or defaults to Intelligence on the Skill Web. The target number is the same as given on the information table. Hacking Pool dice may not be used to supplement this success test roll. Etiquette Test successes can be traded off to reduce the base time for receiving information. Appropriate Contact restrictions do not apply to obtaining information through the Matrix, though the player must indicate what kind of information sources he is searching. If the character is searching corporate-related databases, Corporate Contact information is appropriate. If the character is searching a street-level, chat-line database, Street Contact information is appropriate.

A decker is limited in the number of subjects he can research simultaneously, based on his own abilities and the available time. The maximum number of searches that the decker can conduct at any one time is equal to half the character's Intelligence, divided by 2, rounded up. This base value assumes the decker does nothing else but sit and search, continually adjusting the search paths and parameters. If the character wishes to actively perform other activities, the gamemaster must decide how much time is taken up performing those other activities and adjust the base value accordingly.

SHADOWLAND

The Shadowland network is one particularly wide-ranging and valuable source of information in the Matrix. The decker may only use Shadowland for one request during the course of the adventure, in addition to his other search programs. If the decker wishes to use Shadowland, he must first find a local echo station. To do this, he must make a successful Etiquette (Matrix) (4) Test. Once the decker has located the echo station, he may post a request for information.

The gamemaster then rolls 8 dice against the appropriate target number (listed for each category of information). The gamemaster asks the decker how many of the successes rolled he wishes to allocate to accuracy (more information) or speed (less time). The gamemaster should not tell the decker the number of successes rolled, but instead request the player specify a rough ratio (1 success allocated to accuracy for every 2 to speed, and so on). To determine how long the Shadowland search actually takes, divide the appropriate base time for the search by the number of successes allocated to speed. The average base time for a search in Shadowland is 36 hours. The differing search times needed for certain topics of research are listed after the target number on the **Shadowland** line in each entry. The quotient represents the actual search time, and the successes allocated to accuracy determine the actual information gleaned (consult the **Legwork** tables, as normal).

At some point after the necessary time has passed, the team's decker will find the requested information posted on the Shadowland network. However, the decker has no way of knowing precisely when he can expect the information to turn up. Deckers posting requests on the Shadowland network should check every so often after the minimum elapsed time for the requested information. Once it shows up, the gamemaster uses the accuracy successes to tell the decker how much information is on the network for him.

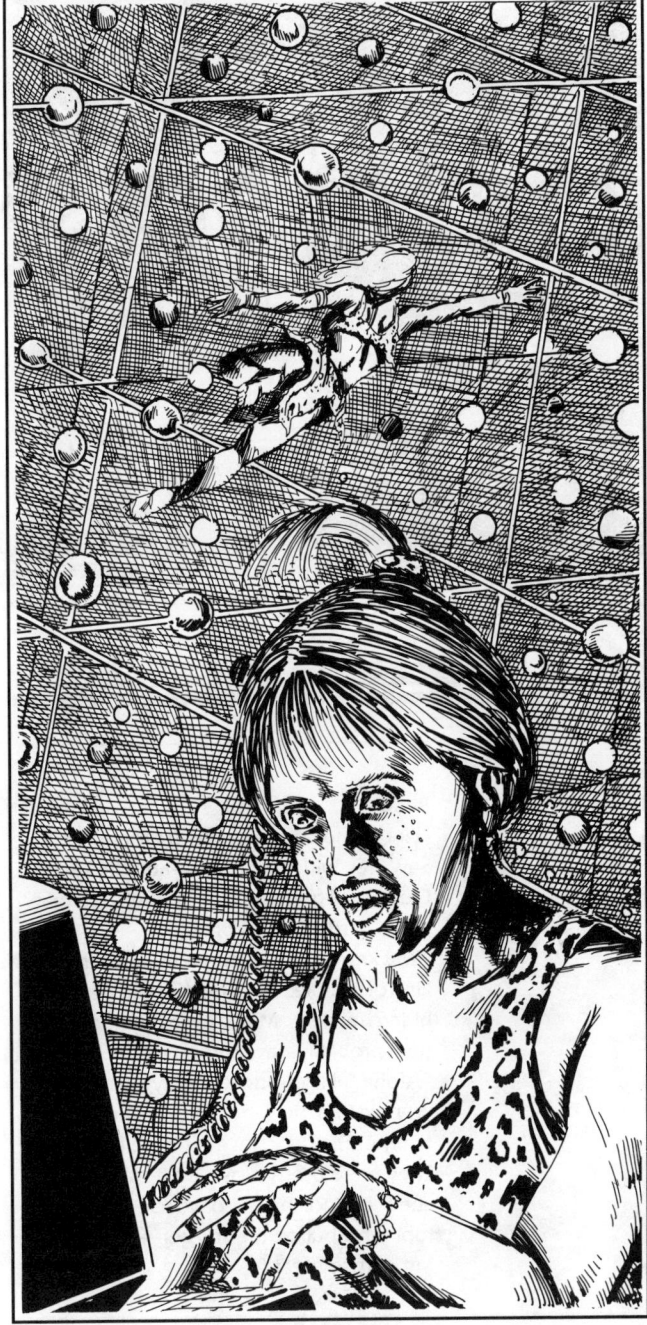

LEGWORK

PEOPLE

The runners can obtain information about the following individuals in the course of this adventure.

ALPHA BLUE

Appropriate Contacts (Target Number 4)
Any Bartender, Fixer, Mr. Johnson, or Street Doc contact.

Shadowland
Target Number 4/Search Time 12 hours

Successes	Result
1	"Her name comes up from time to time. Saw her with some drek-hot decker at Club Ennui trying to look like fluff, but that girl is hard as they come."
2	"You know her? I heard she was in some kind of trouble. Word on the street is she's hiring muscle. Might want to look her up—probably pays top nuyen."
3+	"Alpha? High-priced bodyguard. I've worked with her lab rat brother from time to time. The poor slot got himself geeked. They were pretty close, so it's a sure bet she'll be looking for payback. I pity the fool who pulled the trigger—he's walking corpse meat."

CLEAN STEVE

Appropriate Contacts (Target Number 5)
Any Elven Hitman, Mr. Johnson, or Yakuza Boss.

Shadowland
Target Number 4/Search Time 18 hours

Successes	Result
1	"The name sounds familiar. I think he works uptown as some kind of trigger man, but I wouldn't swear to it."
2	"Top gun—word is he stays clear of enhancements, but don't let that fool you. He's effective and thorough, a pro all the way. Stay clear of Steve and his crew."
3+	"Heard he did some heavy work recently. A real smash-and-burn, but I got no idea what."

DUTCH DONOVAN

Dutch Donovan is the hotshot processor specialist who designed the deliberately flawed Multitech MPCP chip. The runners can ask who Dutch is and where he might be found. Of course, answering the first question is much easier than answering the second. To reflect this fact, the target numbers for discovering Dutch's whereabouts are higher than for general information about him. The first target numbers and success table below apply to general information about Dutch, the second to information about his current location.

Appropriate Contacts (Target Number 6)
Any Decker, corporate scientist or researcher.

Shadowland
Target Number 4/Search Time 24 hours

Successes	Result
1	"Dutch Donovan? Yeah, I know the name. He's a drek-hot chip forger. Can't remember who he works for, though."
2	"Donovan's a genius. He's a master at back-engineering: tell him the result you want and he'll make the chip that'll do it."
3+	"Dutch is a real company man. Loves the perks, loves being valued. Not a real technomancer."

LEGWORK

Appropriate Contacts (Target Number 8)

Any corporate contact (–2 if the contact is connected to a multinational that makes microtronics)

Shadowland

Target Number 6/Search Time 24 hours

Successes	Result
1–2	"He's with Multitech in Bellevue, right? I hear something's up, though, and he might be on a deadline or something. He's pretty much dropped out of sight. He lives in the Smallville complex. It's a Multitech-run corporate housing plot, so watch yourself."
3+	"One ear tells me he's here in Seattle, the other says he's been moved to Shanghai so the bosses can keep an eye on him. Flip a coin, chummer."

ERIN SCOTT

If the runners check on Alpha Blue's real name, they learn Erin Scott "died" in a car crash six years ago. Officially, no kin survived her.

GRIFFIN MOORE

If the runners check SeaSource™, they find an obituary for Griffin Moore, a quality control inspector at Multitech (a local microtronic chip design company). The obit reports that Moore died in a car accident several weeks ago and was interred at the Hammond Necroplex. The obit mentions no immediate family.

Appropriate Contacts (Target Number 8)

Any corporate or technology-related contact (–2 if contact is associated with a multinational that makes microtronics)

Shadowland

Target Number 8/Search Time 18 hours

Successes	Result
1	"Griff works for Multitech Design. Can't think what department, though. Nice guy, real conscientious."
2	"He was a quality controller. Made sure everything was up to spec and straight-straight. Major anal, though."
3+	"He checked the top-shelf stuff—megacorp special orders, mil-spec stuff. Claimed he knew about stuff that would chill your heart. Bet he did, too."

IRON LEGION

The runners can learn different information about the Iron Legion, depending on the questions they ask. The first of the following two tables applies if the runners ask who the Iron Legion gang is; the second applies if they ask where to find the gangers. Target numbers and contacts remain the same for both questions.

Appropriate Contacts (Target Number 5)

Any Gang Boss, Street Cop, or Troll Bouncer.

Shadowland

Target Number 5/Search Time 20 hours

Successes	Result
1	"Lowlife thugs with a jones for guns and cyberware, but no cred to jack the knife. I hear they wear castoff shells and vacuform cosmetics with their synthleathers. Don't know why you'd want anything to do with those slots."
2	"Last night someone cornered the Legion in a blind alley. Geeked most of the gang in one fell swoop. Heard it was a real mess."
3+	"The buzz says Clean Steve geeked 'em." (Depending on who the contact is and how well he knows the characters, he may insist on a payoff up front for this information. If Steve gets wind that the contact turned rat, he may very well ice the slot.)

EYE WITNESS 63

LEGWORK

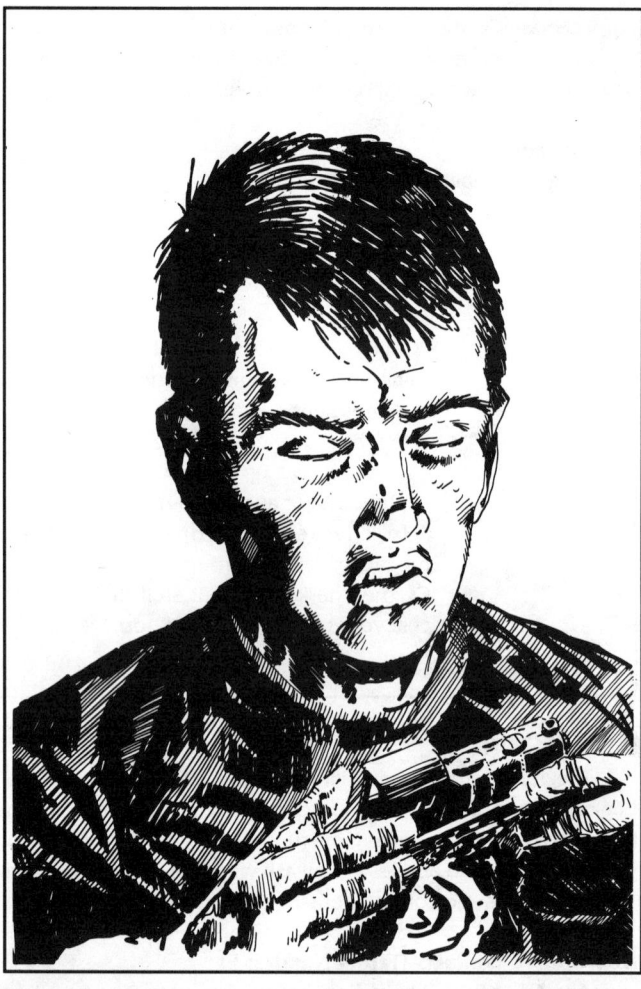

Successes	Result
1+	"The Legion moves with the blitz club Route 66. Don't tell anybody I told ya, but it's going to be at the Brighton Mall tonight…"

NEIL SCOTT

Appropriate Contacts (Target Number 4)
Any Fixer, Mr. Johnson, or technology-oriented contact.

Shadowland
Target Number 4/Search Time 12 hours

Successes	Result
1	"Neil Scott? Know the name… some kinda technofreak, ain't he?"
2+	"A technology analyst, if I recall correctly. Nice guy, straight shooter. Cared more about his toys than anything else."

"RAT" VANIAN

Appropriate Contacts (Target Number 4)
Any Bartender, Dwarf Technician, or Fixer.

Shadowland
Target Number 3/Search Time 12 hours

Successes	Result
1	"Rat trades in all kinds of exotic tech. If you're looking for something you can't find anywhere else, he probably has two in his back room. Don't know how he manages to duck the badge, but he's kept a storefront for four years. Always looking for an angle, but he always keeps his word—a pretty straight shooter for a vulture. His store's in Redmond."
2+	"I hear his shop is closed. Don't know why or for how long, but it can't be a good sign. Hope he pulls through. It would be a shame to lose the only reliable source for dum-dums in town."

PLACES AND EVENTS

The runners can discover information about the following places and events during the course of this adventure.

AGRIPPA AND ASSOCIATES

SeaSource™ identifies Agrippa and Associates as a Puyallup-based waste management and removal company with a hefty chunk of city and private contracts. The entry contains no further information on the privately held firm.

Appropriate Contacts (Target Number 4)
Any City Official or organized-crime contact.

Shadowland
Target Number 4/Search Time 12 hours

Successes	Result
1	"Weird company, Agrippa. Low payroll, but lots of output. They're very mechanized, I hear. Very efficient."
2	"A chummer of mine tried to get work there and they just laughed. He didn't get the joke."
3+	"Have you ever seen their place in Puyallup? Nobody ever goes in or out. I guess the employees live there. Considering what the company does, that may be just as well."

BERKLEY MANAGEMENT

Appropriate Contacts (Target Number 5)
Any City Official, corporate or finance-related contact.

Shadowland
Target Number 4/Search Time 18 hours

Successes	Result
1	"Berkley's a real-estate management and holding company. Don't know much beyond that. I couldn't even say what they manage or hold."
2+	"Yeah, I know 'em. They're the real-estate holders for Agrippa and Associates, the waste removal company. They do a lot of work for the city."

THE CYBEREYE

If the runners acquire Griffin Moore's cybereye from Rat Vanian, they can trace its owner by the serial number on the eye. This task is not easy by any means: the runners' best bet is to post a request for info on the Shadowland network.

Appropriate Contacts (Target Number 6)
Any Street Doc.

Shadowland
Target Number 5/Search Time 20 hours

Successes	Result
1+	"The eye's assigned to a gent named Griffin Moore. Sorry, but that's all I have. I don't get many requests about who owns a piece of cyberware."

HAMMOND NECROPLEX

If the runners consult SeaSource™, they learn that Hammond Necroplex is a mortuary, crematorium and interment site in Renton. The SeaSource™ entry also includes the necroplex's address, telecomm number, and a brief news article about a gas leak on the premises that killed thirteen people a few weeks ago. No further public information is available, but they can learn more about the deaths by doing additional legwork (see following entry).

HAMMOND MASSACRE

The tomb spirit residing in the necroplex wreaked a terrible vengeance once it realized what the director was doing with the corpses in his care. The company's statement on the matter is public record. The truth is not.

Appropriate Contacts (Target Number 4)
Any City Official, Media Producer, or Street Cop.

Shadowland
Target Number 5/Search Time 20 hours

LEGWORK

Successes	Result
1	"The way I remember it, some kinda gas leak killed everyone working there that night. Rumor has it the corpses were pale as ghosts. Real spooky drek."
2–3	"Most people bought the gas leak story. Don't know about you, but *I* never heard of no gas leak that could kill thirteen people on four different floors of a twelve-story building. Have no idea what it was, and I don't want to know."
4+	"You'd be wise to steer clear of the place. Informed sources tell me the place has a bit of magic about it, and whatever killed those people was definitely not human."

MULTITECH

The runners can discover different information on Multitech from public and private sources. Note, however, that Multitech is a tough nut to crack. As a company that builds and designs custom, high-performance, high-cost computer chips for unique or proprietary systems used by some of the biggest megacorps, Multitech has ultra-heavy security.

The runners can obtain the following, public information from SeaSource™ for a small download fee.

Multitech International
Home Office: Shanghai
President/CEO: Jonathon Ki Won
Principal Divisions
Division Name: Multitech Design/Seattle, UCAS
   Division Head: Maximilian Stern
   Chief Products/Services: Custom-chip design and production primarily serving the microtronic industry.

Note: Multitech maintains extensive R&D and fiscal connections with most of the major microtronic megacorporations. As a result, Multitech's physical and Matrix security ratings are considered extremely high, though both remain undocumented.

Additional Information

Appropriate Contacts (Target Number 4)
Any corporate contact or Fixer.

Shadowland
Target Number 5/Search Time 20 hours

Successes	Result
1	"Multitech's a pretty prestigious design and development house. They're very well respected in the industry."
2	"They're a hard company, very demanding of their employees. Work there, though, and you'll be well rewarded. As long as you don't frag up, of course."
3+	"Something's going on over there—lots of nervous bosses back at the home office. I couldn't tell you what, though."

Corporate Profile

For gamemasters using **Corporate Shadowfiles**, Multitech International's profile as of January 1, 2055 is as follows:

Home Office: Shanghai
President/CEO: Jonathon Ki Won
Chairman of the Board: Sir Peter Mathews
Corporate Status: Private Corporation

NET RATING: 59

Major Interests:
   Computer Engineering: 5
   Computer Science: 8
   Consumer Goods: 2
   Cybernetics: 3
   Military Technology: 6

Operations:
   Fiscal: 8
   Intelligence: 7
   Management: 6
   Reputation: 6
   Security: 8
      Magic: 5
      Matrix: 8
      Physical: 10

Military: None Documented

EYE WITNESS

CAST OF SHADOWS

The following NPCs play principal roles in the story of **Eye Witness**. Because they will likely appear more than once in the course of the adventure, their statistics and descriptions are grouped here for convenience. Descriptions and statistics for other, minor NPCs are supplied in the encounters where they appear.

ALPHA BLUE

Born Erin Scott, Alpha Blue learned to fight at an early age. She went on to become a street samurai, earning a name for herself during a short stint as a bodyguard for the superstar Velvet. Her employment with Velvet ended after a skillwire scandal cut short the simsense star's career.

During her career as a high-profile bodyguard Alpha favored blue leather bodysuits, but these days she is more likely to wear a light jacket over spandex. She often sports a black holster and heavy pistol.

Attributes
    Body: 4
    Quickness: 5
    Strength: 4
    Charisma: 4
    Intelligence: 5
    Willpower: 4
    Essence: 2
    Reaction: 5 (9)

Initiative: 9 + 3D6
Threat/Professional Rating: 6/3
Skills
    Armed Combat (Edged Weapons): 4
    Athletics (Running): 5
    Biotech (First Aid): 3
    Car (Passenger Vehicle): 4
    City Speak: 5
    Etiquette (Street): 5
    Firearms (Pistols): 5
    Japanese: 4
    Negotiation (Bargain): 4
    Stealth (Urban): 4
    Throwing Weapons (Non-Aerodynamic): 4
    Unarmed Combat (Cyber Implant Weaponry): 6

Cyberware
    Retractable Razors
    Smartlink
    Wired Reflexes: 2

Gear
    Armor Clothing: 0/3
    Browning Max-Power [Heavy Pistol, 10 (clip), SA, 9M, w/2 extra clips, Silencer, External Smartgun]
    Credstick (w/2,000-nuyen balance)
    Personal Computer (Pocket model w/Printer)
    Portable Phone (Handset Unit)
    Stimulant Patches (2 of Rating 3, 1 of Rating 5)
    Trauma Patch
    White Noise Generator

CONDITION MONITOR

	LIGHT STUN	MODERATE STUN	SERIOUS STUN		DEADLY STUN
STUN	+1 TN# / -1 Init.	+2 TN# / -2 Init.	+3 TN# / -3 Init.		Unc.
PHYSICAL	+1 TN# / -1 Init.	+2 TN# / -2 Init.	+3 TN# / -3 Init.		Unc. maybe dead
	LIGHT WOUND	MODERATE WOUND	SERIOUS WOUND		DEADLY WOUND

CAST OF SHADOWS

CLEAN STEVE

Clean Steve is a rare breed, a drek-hot assassin who has risen to the top of his profession without the benefit of cyberware. After faulty cyber enhancements caused his brother's death, Steve committed himself to years of martial arts training that have left him a match for most samurai.

An extremely handsome young man with light blonde hair and clear blue eyes, Steve wears a white turtleneck and a dark blazer unless he is on a run where stealth is necessary. Though a master of unarmed combat techniques, he occasionally carries a gun in a concealed shoulder holster.

Attributes
  Body: 5
  Quickness: 6
  Strength: 5
  Charisma: 5
  Intelligence: 6
  Willpower: 5
  Essence: 6
  Reaction: 6
Initiative: 6 + 1D6
Threat/Professional Rating: 8/4
Skills
  Armed Combat: 5
  Athletics: 5
  Bike (Two-wheeler): 5
  Biotech (First Aid): 4
  Computer: 4
  Etiquette (Street): 6
  Firearms (Pistols): 6
  Interrogation (Verbal): 5
  Leadership (Military): 5
  Negotiation: 5
  Stealth (Urban): 5
  Unarmed Combat (Martial Arts Style): 7
Gear
  Ares Predator [Heavy Pistol, 15 (clip), SA, 9M, Explosive Rounds, Laser Sight (-1 modifier to target numbers)]
  Armor Clothing: 0/3
  Credstick (w/5,000-nuyen balance)
  Portable Phone (Earplug Unit w/Booster Pack and Pocket Secretary)

"RAT" VANIAN

Vanian buys and sells used tech, no questions asked. His shop is a regular stop for runners on their way into or out of town.

A middle-aged human with long hair and a shaggy beard, Rat rarely leaves his workshop, and dresses in layers of rumpled clothes whose pockets are stuffed with high-tech odds and ends.

Attributes
  Body: 4
  Quickness: 4
  Strength: 3
  Charisma: 5
  Intelligence: 6
  Willpower: 4
  Essence: 6
  Reaction: 5
Initiative: 5 + 1D6
Threat/Professional Rating: 2/2
Skills
  Computer (Hardware): 4
  Computer Theory (Hardware): 4
  Cybertechnology (Bodyware): 4
  Electronics: 5
  Etiquette (Street): 5
  Firearms (Pistols): 3
  Negotiation (Bargain): 6
Cyberware
  Wired Reflexes: 2

CONDITION MONITOR

	LIGHT STUN	MODERATE STUN	SERIOUS STUN		DEADLY STUN
STUN	+1 TN# -1 Init.	+2 TN# -2 Init.	+3 TN# -3 Init.		Unc.
PHYSICAL	+1 TN# -1 Init.	+2 TN# -2 Init.	+3 TN# -3 Init.		Unc. maybe dead
	LIGHT WOUND	MODERATE WOUND	SERIOUS WOUND		DEADLY WOUND

CAST OF SHADOWS

Gear
- Credstick (w/2,500-nuyen balance)
- Micro-Recorder
- Personal Computer (Pocket model w/Printer)
- Portable Phone (Handset Unit)

Attributes
- Body: 5
- Quickness: 3
- Strength: 4
- Charisma: 4
- Intelligence: 5
- Willpower: 6
- Essence: 5
- Reaction: 4

Initiative: 4 + 1D6
Threat/Professional Rating: 6/3
Powers
- Enhanced Senses (Improved Hearing and Smell)

Weaknesses
- Allergy (Sunlight, Mild)
- Reduced Senses (Blind)

Skills
- Firearms (Pistol): 3
- Etiquette (Corporate): 6
- Etiquette (Street): 6
- Leadership: 7
- Negotiation (Bargain): 5
- Psychology (Group Behavior): 4

Gear
- Browning Max-Power [Heavy Pistol, 10 (clip), SA, 9M]
- Personal Computer (Wrist model w/Printer)
- Voice Mask: 5

ADAM SHEPHERD

Born Eric Steward, heir to a corp fortune, Shepherd had the bad luck to goblinize into a ghoul. Fortunately for him, he managed to maintain his sanity, and used his considerable intelligence to amass millions of nuyen under the assumed name of Adam Shepherd. Shepherd looks like a typical businessman at first glance, but closer inspection reveals something not quite right about him. His lightly scarred face has the peculiar sheen left by extensive plastic surgery, and his expensive suits do not seem to sit right on his gangly frame. Those who get close to him notice that his heavy cologne masks a peculiar odor.

EYE WITNESS

PLAYER HANDOUT #1

BABY BLUE—

I GOT BURNED BAD OR YOU WOULDN'T BE READING THIS. KNEW IT WOULD HAPPEN SOONER OR LATER—I'D HOPED IT WOULD BE LATER. JUST ANOTHER PROFESSIONAL HAZARD AND ALL THAT—YOU OF ALL PEOPLE SHOULD UNDERSTAND.

IT ALL STARTED WHEN MY FRIEND AND BEST CUSTOMER VANIAN PAID ME A VISIT. HE BROUGHT A BLUEPRINT (HE MAY BE A DREK-HOT FENCE, BUT HE IS NO TECHNOMANCER) AND ASKED ME TO SCOPE IT. HE WANTED TO KNOW WHAT THE FRAGGIN' THING WAS AND WHAT HE COULD GET FOR IT.

NO PROBLEM—OR SO I THOUGHT.

WHEN I GOT TO WORK ON THE BLUEPRINT, THE FIRST THING I DID WAS LOOK FOR THE R&D STAMP THAT WOULD TAG THE COMPANY THAT COMMISSIONED THE WORK. NO LUCK—THE BLUEPRINT MUST HAVE BEEN STRIPPED OR SCANNED, BECAUSE THE EDGES OF THE IMAGE WERE SO BADLY DISTORTED THAT NOT EVEN MY HEURISTIC ENHANCERS COULD RESURRECT THE FRAGGING CODES.

NEXT, I BEGAN TO WORK UP A COMPARISON FILE, LOOKING FOR ANY TELLTALE DESIGN FLOURISHES IN THE CHIP THAT MIGHT TAG IT AS THE WORK OF A SPECIFIC DESIGNER. AFTER A FEW HOURS I FINALLY CAME UP WITH A MATCH—A JOKER NAMED DUTCH DONOVAN, A REAL WIZBOY. MY RECORDS SHOW HIM STUCK IN R&D AT MULTITECH. SO NOW WE KNOW WHO DREW THIS BABY.

THEN I WENT ON TO THE HARD PART—TRYING TO FIGURE OUT WHAT THE FRAGGIN' BLUEPRINT IS FOR. IT WAS OBVIOUSLY PART OF A DESIGN FOR AN OPTICAL CHIP, BUT DETERMINING WHAT THAT CHIP MIGHT BE USED FOR IS ALMOST IMPOSSIBLE WITHOUT SEEING THE ENTIRE DESIGN. IT'S LIKE LOOKING AT A LENGTH OF WIRE. SORT OF. ANYWAY, HERE'S WHERE THE TROUBLE STARTS. YOU SEE, I FOUND WHAT LOOKS LIKE AN INTENTIONAL REROUTE AROUND A NONCRITICAL SUBPROCESSING NODE. I KNOW—IN ENGLISH. WHAT IT MEANS, OR COULD MEAN, IS THAT THE DESIGN WOULD ELIMINATE EXPENSIVE MANUFACTURING AND REDUCE PROGRAMMING TIME. AND THAT WOULD CUT COSTS DRASTICALLY, BUT ALSO CREATE AN INFERIOR CHIP.

SO HERE I AM WITH A BLUEPRINT THAT MAY PROVE THAT A MAJOR MULTINATIONAL IS RIPPING OFF THEIR CUSTOMERS BY SHORTCUTTING THEIR SUBCONTRACTS. I'M TEMPTED TO DUMP THE WHOLE SLOTTING MESS BACK IN VANIAN'S LAP, BUT IF HE DECIDES TO ROLL OVER IT WOULD LEAVE ME HIGH AND DRY. IF MY LUCK HOLDS OUT, I'LL FIGURE A WAY OUT OF THIS AND YOU WILL NEVER GET THIS LETTER. IF I DON'T, THIS IS GOODBYE.

SEE YOU ON THE OTHER SIDE,

Neil

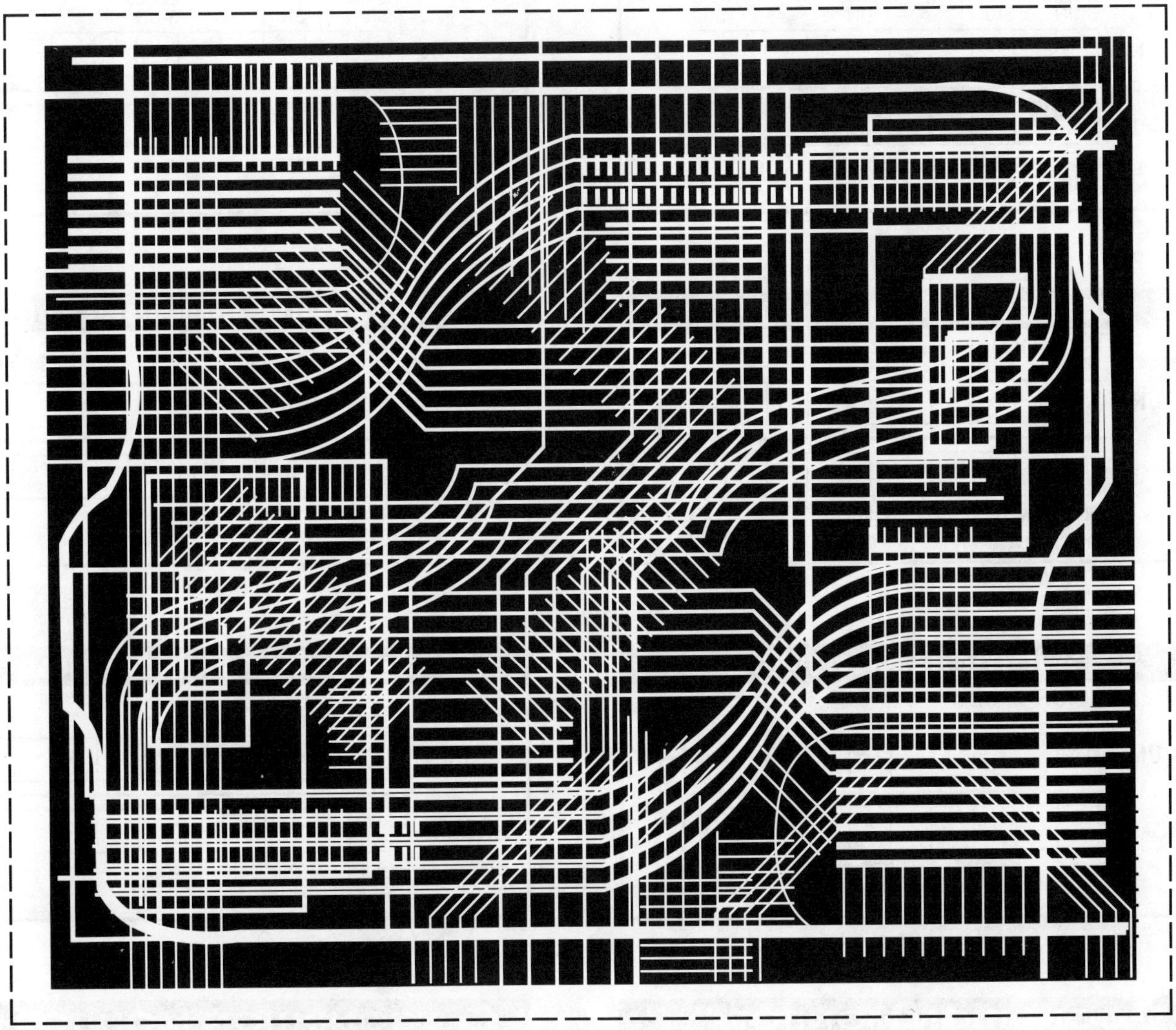

PLAYER HANDOUTS

PLAYER HANDOUT #2

PLAYER HANDOUT #3

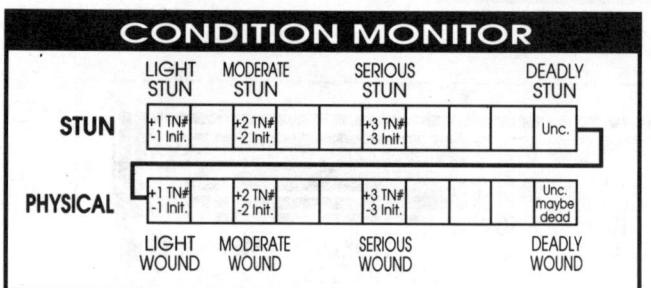